ENGLISH G

W0272832

Liebe Schülerin, lieber Schüler!

Die Hörtexte für die *Listening*-Aufgaben sowie Mustertexte für die *Speaking*-Aufgaben findest du online unter www.cornelsen.de/webcodes.

Gib dort den Webcode LH-5-KAT-AUDIO ein und lade die Dateien herunter.

Das Kopfhörersymbol mit Track-Nummer im Heft zeigt dir an, welchen Hörtext du für die Aufgabe anhören musst.

5

LIGHTHOUSE

Klassenarbeitstrainer

für Schülerinnen und Schüler

mit Lösungen und Lerntipps

Cornelsen

English G | LIGHTHOUSE **5** Klassenarbeitstrainer

Erarbeitet von: Bärbel Schweitzer, Staufen

In Zusammenarbeit mit der Englischredaktion: Klaus Unger (Projektleitung); Cornelia Frisse (verantwortliche Redakteurin); Nicola Regner

Beratende Mitwirkung: Matthias Teschner, Bad Schwartau

Illustrationen: Karen Donnelly, Brighton (S. 15 (u. 59); S. 51)

Cover-Illustration: Dorina Tessmann, Berlin

Layoutkonzept: Klein & Halm Grafikdesign, Berlin

Umschlaggestaltung: Cornelsen Schulverlage Design unter Verwendung der Entwürfe von Klein & Halm Grafikdesign, Berlin und kleiner und bold, Berlin

Layout und technische Umsetzung: Buch und Gestaltung, Britta Dieterle, Berlin

www.cornelsen.de

1. Auflage, 5. Druck 2021

Druck: H. Heenemann, Berlin

ISBN 978-3-06-032383-8

Inhalt

Vorwort

Here we go!
Vor dir liegt dein Klassenarbeitstrainer.
Für jede Unit findest du zwei Klassenarbeiten, die dich gezielt beim Üben unterstützen.

Plane genügend Zeit für die Vorbereitung auf die Klassenarbeit ein. Sobald du weißt, was in der Klassenarbeit drankommt, kannst du deinen Lernplan erstellen. Am Ende des Heftes findest du einen Beispiel-Lernplan und Pläne zum Selbstausfüllen.

Datum der Klassenarbeit:	12. November
Was kommt dran?	Unit 2 (Listening, Mediation, Writing, Vokabeln, *indirect speech*)

Datum	Was ich lernen will	Erledigt?	Was ich noch einmal wiederholen muss / wichtige Hinweise
30.10.	Lernplan erstellen	✓	
31.10.	Vokabeln Unit 2 wiederholen (S. 213 – 215)	✓	Blaue Box zu *agree*!

Eine ☞ vor einer Aufgabe zeigt dir **Tipps für das Lösen einer Aufgabe** an. Fühlst du dich bereits sicher, kannst du diese Tipps auch abdecken.

***More help*-Aufgaben** bieten dir zusätzliche Hilfen an. Du findest sie am Ende des Heftes. Achtung: Wenn du *More help* in Anspruch nimmst, erhältst du weniger Punkte! Trage deine Punktzahl dann vorne bei der Klassenarbeit ein.

Die **Hörtexte** für die *Listening*-Aufgaben sowie **Mustertexte** für die *Speaking*-Aufgaben findest du **online** unter **www.cornelsen.de/webcodes**. Gib dort den Webcode **LH-5-KAT-AUDIO** ein und lade die Dateien herunter. Das Kopfhörersymbol mit Track-Nummer im Heft zeigt dir an, welchen Hörtext du für die Aufgabe anhören musst. Nimm das Gesprochene auf, dann kannst du dich im Anschluss mithilfe des Lösungsvorschlags gut überprüfen.

Im **Lösungsheft** in der Mitte deines Klassenarbeitstrainers findest du alle Lösungen, die Hörtexte für die *Listening*-Aufgaben sowie nützliche Lerntipps, die dich beim weiteren Lernen unterstützen. Der **Punkteschlüssel** vorne im Heft hilft dir, deinen Lernstand einzuschätzen.

Übrigens: Die Klassenarbeiten in diesem Heft prüfen das Gelernte sehr ausführlich ab. Du kannst sie dir also gerne auch in kleinere Portionen einteilen.

All the best for you!
Bärbel Schweitzer

Gesamtpunktzahl ______/72 Note ______

1 READING A window on my life

South Sydney High School Magazine

Ⓐ Hi, I'm Paul, I'm 25 years old and I used to be a student at this school, just like you are now. Riley and Olivia asked me to give you a window on my life and write something about my career as a photographer. I'm very happy to do it!

Ⓑ It all started when I was fifteen and won a photo competition with one of my Sydney photos. I've always taken lots of photos – photos of my family, birthday parties, holidays, all kinds of photos really. But what I loved most was walking around Sydney and taking pictures of my favourite spots. What a happy day it was when one of my photos was in a big Australian photo magazine! I won a camera which allowed me to take better quality photos.

Ⓒ When I finished school I thought about becoming a professional photographer. To turn my hobby into a job – what an exciting idea! But would I make enough money to live on? After discussing with my parents, friends and with the job centre people, I finally decided to play it safe and get a bread-and-butter job in a bank.

Ⓓ Of course I kept taking photos, and I started focusing on two topics: my hometown Sydney and travel. Every year I made calendars with my best photos for friends and family. Some of them liked their calendars so much, they bought copies as presents for their friends. It's not that I didn't like my job at the bank, but I started thinking again about becoming a professional photographer. But how? Surely I couldn't live off the calendars that I sold once a year. So I kept working at the bank, I kept taking photographs and I kept thinking about my dream.

Ⓔ One day I started selling my photos on the internet. There are millions of photos on the internet that you can buy and download, so I didn't expect much. But one photo that I had taken on a trip to Bali really stood out – it became my first real success. I didn't become a millionaire, but one of my photos earned me money! So that year I made my new calendar with my Bali photos and sent a copy to a few calendar businesses. Most of them weren't interested, but suddenly – there it was: an offer for a photo project about Sydney, my hometown. What luck! That was three years ago and the beginning of my professional career. I kept working at the bank and did the photo projects too.

Ⓕ Working two jobs at the same time was challenging. But my photos were successful, so one year ago I took the risk and gave up my job at the bank to become a professional photographer. It's definitely not an easy job. I had to learn how to manage my own business. I would advise everybody who's thinking of having his or her own business to do the same thing – it's important. Anyway – today I have my own business and I'm proud of it.

Sydney Harbour Bridge

A beach in Bali

a) Read the text and answer the questions. ____/12

1 Why did Riley and Olivia choose Paul for the article?

____ (2 P)

2 Why didn't Paul become a photographer as soon as he left school?

____ (2 P)

3 What fact shows that his calendars were very successful?

____ (2 P)

4 What helped Paul with his dream of becoming a professional photographer? (two facts)

____

____ (4 P)

5 What's important when you become a professional and have your own business?

____ (2 P)

b) Read the text again. Then underline the best heading for each paragraph. ____/6

Ⓐ Why I became a photographer / About me / My life as a student at South Sydney High

Ⓑ First steps / Favourite places in Sydney / Why I won the competition

Ⓒ My parents say "no" / My job at the bank / A difficult decision

Ⓓ Successful calendars / Nice friends / Living on very little money

Ⓔ My trip to Bali / Millions of photos! / First job as a photographer

Ⓕ How to run a business / Making a dream come true / Working two jobs

2 WORDS In English, please! ____/6

Was sagst du, wenn du sagen willst, ...

1 *dass es wahrscheinlich regnen wird?*

____

2 *dass nichts mit deinem alten Fahrrad vergleichbar ist?*

____

3 *dass der nächste Supermarkt in der Murray Street ist?*

____

4 *dass es sich lohnt, den neuen Film anzuschauen?*

____

5 *dass ihr euch regelmäßig jeden Freitagnachmittag trefft?*

____

6 *dass Hamid sein Auto überhaupt nicht benutzt?*

____

3 WORDS Corresponding nouns

a) Write four verbs and nouns which are the same. ____/2

	verb	noun
›	*race*	*race*
1		
2		
3		
4		

b) Write four adjectives and their corresponding nouns that end in *-ness*. ____/4

	adjective	noun ending in *-ness*
›	*weak*	*weakness*
1		
2		
3		
4		

c) The corresponding noun of an adjective doesn't always end in *-ness*.
Write the corresponding nouns of these words. ____/2

	adjective	noun
›	*healthy*	*health*
1	careful	
2	central	
3	hot	
4	traditional	

4 LANGUAGE A blog entry from Australia

____/14

Aeden and Grace from the USA are travelling Australia at the moment. Read their blog and fill in the correct tenses. Use the *simple present, present progressive, simple past* and *going-to future*.

Welcome to Aeden and Grace's travel blog!

Home | Contact | About us | **Blog**

Day 3 – Exploring Sydney

Hi guys, here we are again!

On our tour through Australia we ____________________ (do) something special every day, well, nearly every day! On Monday we ________________ (arrive) here in Sydney and in the afternoon we ____________________ (not do) anything but sleep. But yesterday ________________ (be) different. As you know, we love adventures, and so we ____________________ (decide) not to go on one of those commercial sightseeing tours. Instead, we ________________ (want) to explore the city on our own and on foot. So yesterday evening our feet ________________ (hurt) quite a bit, but we ________________ (be) full of exciting impressions of this amazing city. Just have a look at our photos!

At the moment we __________________________ (have) some sandwiches in Hyde Park. Sightseeing ____________________ (make) you hungry! We __________________ (not go) to a restaurant every day – it's too expensive. Later we ____________________________ (visit) the 309 m high Sydney Tower Eye, and we ____________________________ (look forward to) the great view. We ____________________________ (post) some photos from up there in the next days.

5 MEDIATION Dangers at the beach

____/11

More help p. 57/58

You are staying with a family in Australia for a few months. Today you are at the beach with your Australian family and you meet a German couple (Herr and Frau Koch). They have lots of questions that your host sister, Chloe, tries to answer. You help with the English and the German.

Perspektivwechsel

Bei *Mediation*-Aufgaben musst du beachten, für wen du sprichst. Die folgende Situation soll dir dies verdeutlichen:

Du bist mit Fabian, einem deutschen Freund, in Australien am Strand. Fabian möchte ein Surfboard leihen und bittet dich, ihm zu helfen.

Fabian: Sag der Frau vom Verleih bitte, dass ich das Surfboard gerne für den ganzen Tag nehmen möchte.

In diesem Fall musst du auf Englisch vermitteln und sagen:

He*'d like to take the surfboard for the whole day.* – und nicht:
I*'d like to take ...*, denn du möchtest das Surfboard ja nicht leihen.

Frau Koch *Wir sind erst gestern angekommen und haben ein paar Fragen. Gibt es irgendwelche Sicherheitsvorschriften, die wir am Strand beachten müssen?*

Du ______________________________

____

______________________________ (2 P)

Chloe Well, the sea at some of the most famous beaches can be very dangerous. But there are lifeguards at these beaches, so you should always stay near them. Also you should watch the flags: always swim in the area between the red and the yellow flags. That's the safest area.

Du ______________________________

____

____

______________________________ (3 P)

Frau Koch *Und wie ist es mit den Haien? Wir haben schon etwas Angst vor Haiangriffen.*

Du ______________________________ (1 P)

Chloe Again you should only swim at beaches with lifeguards. Never swim in the dark, or in the early morning. Don't swim too far out into the sea and don't swim near rivers.

Du ______________________________

____

______________________________ (2 P)

Herr Koch *Was müssen wir noch beachten?*

Du ______________________________ (1 P)

Chloe The sun is very strong in Australia. So always protect your skin with strong suncream, wear a hat and long shirts. You shouldn't stay out in the sun the whole day.

Du ______________________________

____

______________________________ (2 P)

Frau Koch *Puh, da muss man schon auf einiges aufpassen. Aber ich danke euch beiden ganz herzlich für eure Hilfe.*

Du *Bitte, gern geschehen.* Thanks for your help, Chloe.

6 SPEAKING Your 'Bundesland' – a place to visit? ____/15

1 Listen to Jack. He's talking about 'his' state Western Australia.

Now you

Give a short talk about your 'Bundesland' in Germany. What makes it interesting and different for visitors? Make a mindmap first. Speak for about three minutes.

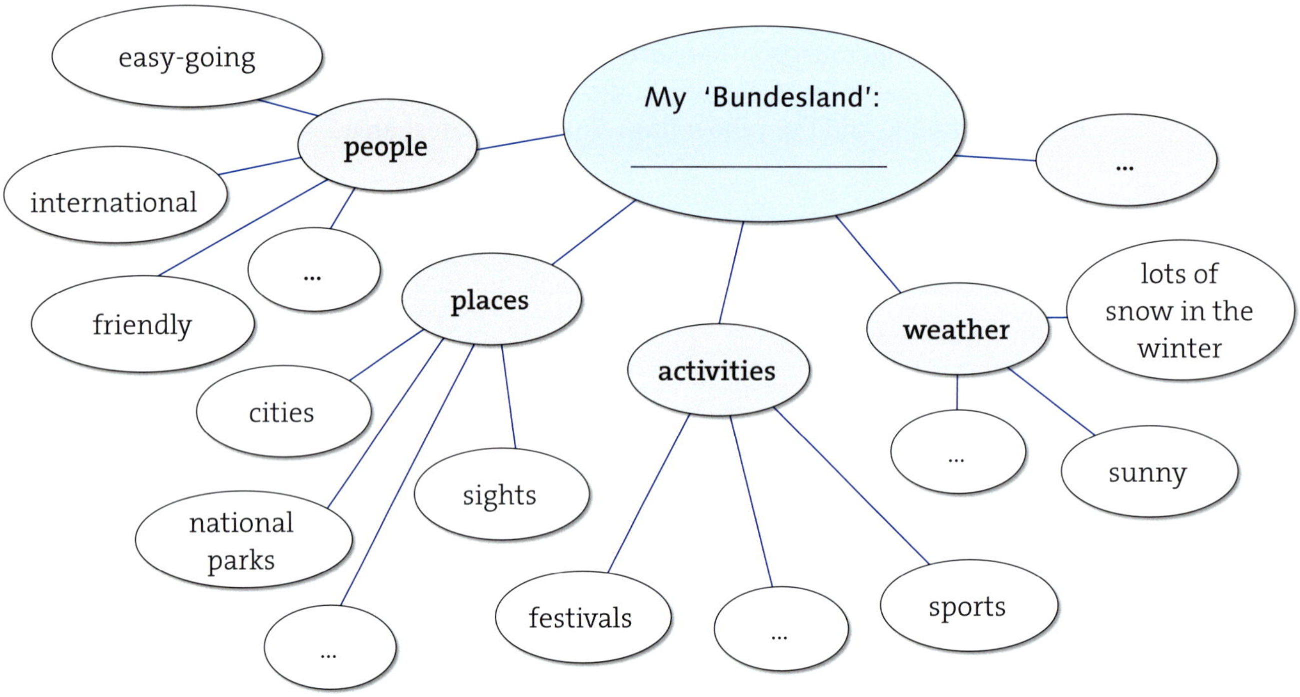

Klassenarbeit B

Unit 1

Gesamtpunktzahl ______/57 Note ______

1 LISTENING Winter in Australia

2 **a)** Listen to the radio programme. Then tick (✓) the correct sentence. ______/1

1	The programme is about the advantages and disadvantages of winter in Australia.	
2	The programme promises a good winter in Australia.	
3	The programme informs about winter in Australia.	

3 **b)** Listen to the first part of the radio programme again. Then tick (✓) the best sentence endings. ______/5

1	In Canberra ...	it snows very often.	
		it hasn't snowed for many years.	
		it has never snowed before.	
2	People in Canberra ...	sent round the news quickly.	
		don't like the snow.	
		were surprised about the snow.	
3	There were problems in Canberra because ...	snowball fights got out of control.	
		some kangaroos died in the cold.	
		there were dangerous fires.	
4	The snow in Canberra ...	started during the day.	
		wasn't dangerous for traffic.	
		stopped after an hour.	
5	The snow ...	makes it possible to go skiing.	
		usually falls in December.	
		is likely to fall in the desert.	

4 **c)** Listen to the second part of the programme again and tick (✓) right or wrong. ____/7

		right	wrong
1	It snows in the Australian Alps because they are higher than the rest of the country.		
2	In June, temperatures in the Australian Alps go up.		
3	The highest mountain is more than 2000 metres high.		
4	Australians don't like winter sports so much.		
5	Skiing came to Australia about 150 years ago.		
6	Australian kids learn how to ski and snowboard in high school.		
7	Australians don't enjoy the snow because they aren't used to it.		

2 WORDS A crossword

____/10

Find the words and write them into the crossword.

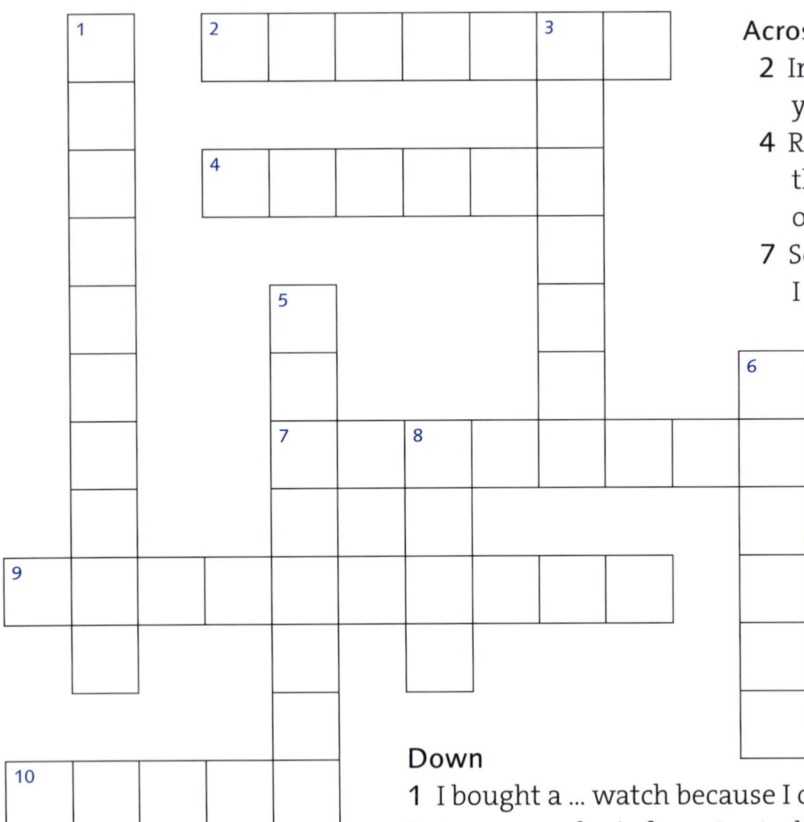

Across
2 In Australia you should always ... your head from the sun.
4 Ruby knows very much about the Australian Alps. She's an ... on them.
7 Some people call me 'Shorty', but I don't like that ... very much.
9 Australia is the smallest of the seven ...
10 Little kids shouldn't stay in the sun too much. It's better for them to play in the ...

Down
1 I bought a ... watch because I often go swimming.
3 A person who is from Australia is an Australian ...
5 This book is great! I'll ... to read it at home.
6 The bite of a dangerous spider can be ...
8 If a boat gets into bad weather it's important to have a good ... on board.

3 WORDS Opposites and synonyms

a) Find the opposites. ____/3

1 narrow ≠ ____________________

2 (to) die ≠ ____________________

3 (the) cold ≠ ____________________

b) Find words or phrases that mean more or less the same. ____/3

1 nearly = ____________________

2 (to) go on = ____________________

3 (to) repair a bike = ____________________

4 LANGUAGE About my classmates

____/7

Think about your classmates and make true sentences about them. Some of your sentences should be positive, some should be negative. Make sure that you use the correct tense.

› like swimming: *Pia doesn't like swimming. (or: Pia likes swimming.)*

1 visit Australia soon: ____________________

____

2 try kangaroo meat: ____________________

____

3 give a talk about Australia last month: ____________________

____

4 be born in Australia: ____________________

5 know a lot about the First Australians: ____________________

____

6 read a book about Australia at the moment: ____________________

____

7 be afraid of sharks: ____________________

5 REVISION **LANGUAGE An interview** ____/6

You meet an Australian student and you want to interview him or her about the Australian winter for your school magazine. Think of six questions you could ask him or her. Use at least three different tenses.

1 ____?

2 ____?

3 ____?

4 ____?

5 ____?

6 ____?

☞ **Fragebildung**

Fragen im *simple present* und im *simple past* bildest du mit dem Hilfsverb *do*:
- *do/does* im *simple present*
- *did* im *simple past*

Beispiele:

simple present	Do you like Chinese food? Where does Shelley meet his team?
simple past	Did you see Jenna yesterday? When did Pete meet her?

Zur Bildung der **anderen Zeiten**, beim Verb *be* und bei den Modalverben (z.B. *can, may, must, should, could*) benötigst du kein Hilfsverb für die Frage.

Beispiele:

present perfect	Have you cleaned your room? Why haven't you finished your homework yet?
present progressive	Is Lucy giving her presentation today? When are you travelling to Spain?
going-to future	Are we going to take another test this week? When is she going to read that book?
will-future	Will the train arrive on time? When will it rain?
Verb *be*	Are you ready? What's your name? Was he in London last week?
Modalverben	Can you help me, please? Why should I let you copy my homework?

6 WRITING Jill's day in the snow

_____/15

More help p. 59

Look at the pictures and imagine you are Jill. Write about the snow in Canberra last week. Write about 120 words.

1

Tuesday evening

2

Wednesday morning

3

At school

4

5

After school

6

Wednesday evening

7

Thursday morning

Drei Tipps für einen gelungenen Text:

1 Achte auf die richtigen Zeiten.

2 Beschreibe Jills Gefühle.

3 Verwende *time phrases* und *linking words.*

You can start like this:

Last Tuesday the weather forecast announced ____________________

Klassenarbeit A

Gesamtpunktzahl ______ /53	Note ______

1 READING Dealing with your feelings

The following text is taken from a brochure[1] for young people about bullying.

Everyone will deal with bullying differently. Some people already have good strategies and don't care so much, but for others the feelings are harder to deal with.

We all need **love, respect** and **understanding** in our lives, we need **friends** and **interests** in and out of school and a place where we belong. These things can make us feel safe and help us to deal with problems. It is important to remember that feeling bad is not forever and things can get better. Everyone in life has hard times, and learning how to work through problems will make you more able to take control of your life.

There are **good ways** and some not so good ways to deal with bullying. Talking to friends or family, doing things you love, listening to music, playing games and staying active are all positive things you can do for yourself. They won't make the bullying stop, but they will help you to **manage your feelings**. Just being listened to can help you to **feel better**, more accepted and less alone; just as listening to a friend can help them to feel better.

Arguing, being aggressive towards others, doing things to hurt yourself, missing school, drinking or smoking, or stopping

communicating with people may seem like **ways to deal with your problems**, but they are not healthy; they don't deal with the bullying or how it makes you feel.

If you don't feel there is anyone you can talk to, or anyone you can be yourself around, it might help to **look for groups** or clubs in your area or online, where you feel you can fit in better. So look out for people or groups that have the same interests as you, groups that you feel represent **you**, groups that make you **feel at home**.

It's **important** to remember that **feeling bad** is **not forever** and **things can get better**.

a) Read the text. Then tick (✓) the sentence that describes the text best. ______ /1

1	The text is about school and bullying.	
2	The text is about why people become bullies.	
3	The text is about how to deal with bullying.	

1 Adapted from: Bullying ... What can I do? (www.respectme.org.uk/cyberbullying.html)

b) Read the text again and tick (✓) right, wrong or not in the text. ____/14

☞ Manchmal fällt es schwer, zwischen *wrong* und *not in the text* zu unterscheiden.
Bei *wrong* ist die Aussage falsch, d.h. es steht anders im Text.
Bei *not in the text* fehlt entweder eine Aussage hierzu im Text ganz oder sie ist nicht so präzise wie in der Aufgabe und wird daher als *not in the text* eingestuft.

		right	wrong	not in the text
1	Everybody has a good strategy against bullying.			
2	Having positive things in your life can help a lot.			
3	Everybody should get at least one compliment a day.			
4	If you respect others, they will respect you.			
5	Every student should learn about bullying at school.			
6	You can fight bullying easily if you know how.			
7	Ignoring the problem is a good way of taking control of your life.			
8	There are different ways of dealing with bullying.			
9	You should look out for healthy ways to get on with the problem.			
10	Staying at home a lot will make you feel better.			
11	It's good to find someone you can talk to.			
12	The internet is not a good place for help.			
13	Think about your hobbies and find people with the same hobbies.			
14	Going to a club once a week can make you feel better.			

2 WORDS Say it in English ____/8

Was sagst du auf Englisch, wenn du sagen willst, …

1 *dass das so ein toller Laden ist?*

____

2 *dass eure Meinung wichtig ist?*

____

3 *dass jemand nicht nerven soll?*

___

4 *dass es dein gutes Recht ist, hier zu sein?*

___

5 *„Übrigens, ich habe eine Rolle im Schultheater bekommen."*

___

6 *dass du ihn davor gewarnt hast, dort hinzugehen?*

___

7 *dass du Paula in letzter Zeit nicht gesehen hast?*

___

8 *dass ihr nicht in allem übereinstimmt?*

___

3 LANGUAGE A class discussion about bullying

a) Here's what some kids said about bullying.
Put their sentences into indirect speech.

____/6

More help p. 60

Indirekte Rede (Aussagesätze und Fragen)

Wenn du einen Aussage- oder Fragesatz aus der direkten Rede in die indirekte Rede setzen willst, musst du zwei Dinge bedenken:

1 In welcher Zeit steht das einleitende Verb? *(say, complain, ask, ...)*
Steht es im *simple past*, so ändern sich die Zeiten in der indirekten Rede *(backshift)*.
2 Muss man Personen (Pronomen) ändern?
Wenn in der direkten Rede ein Pronomen steht, ändert es sich manchmal in der indirekten Rede.

Katie

1 Some of my classmates call me names.

2 Jack and Igor make fun of me.

Ethan

1 *Katie said that* ___

2 *Ethan complained that* ___

Molly

(3) Jessica sometimes kicks me.

(4) I get mean text messages again and again.

Omar

3 *Molly said* ______________________________

4 *Omar* ______________________________

b) This is what the teacher said to the bullies.
Put her sentences into indirect speech.

_____/6

Indirekte Rede (Aufforderungen, Bitten, Ratschläge)

Wenn du Aufforderungen, Bitten oder Ratschläge in die indirekte Rede setzt, musst du die Zeitform nicht verschieben. Du musst aber Folgendes bedenken:

1 Manchmal musst du (wie bei Aussage- und Fragesätzen) die Person (Pronomen) ändern.
2 Indirekte Aufforderungen, Bitten oder Ratschläge werden mit dem Infinitiv gebildet: *(not) to* + Infinitiv.

(1) Kids, don't call Katie names, please.

(2) Jack and Igor, stop making fun of Ethan!

teacher

(3) Jessica, don't kick Molly again!

(4) Don't write mean text messages. Do your homework instead!

1 *The teacher asked* ______________________________

2 *She told* ______________________________

3 *She told* ______________________________

4 *She* ______________________________

and ______________________________

4 MEDIATION About ChildLine

___/12

You are doing a project about bullying at school and have to talk about organizations that help children. Read this text from a brochure[1] about bullying. Then answer the questions below in German.

What can you expect from ChildLine?

When you are having a hard time it can help to talk to someone about what's happening. You can contact ChildLine about anything, no problem is too big or too small.

If you are feeling scared or out of control or just want to talk to someone, you can contact ChildLine.

When you call ChildLine on 0800 1111 or contact us for a one-to-one chat online (www.childline.org.uk) you will be connected to somebody here at ChildLine who will listen to whatever your problem is. This person won't tell you what's right or wrong or make you feel bad – they are someone you can trust.

You don't need to give us your name or any details about yourself if you don't want to. We might ask you some questions to try and understand how you are feeling or to help you talk about it. You don't have to answer them if you don't want to, but by contacting us you have taken the first step to changing things. We will help you think about what needs to change in your life and who might support you to make these changes. This might feel difficult at first, but looking at what needs to be different is important to help stop what is happening to you.

You can get back in touch with us at any time, even if you didn't tell us anything the first time you contacted us.

You can also contact us by sending an email or posting on the ChildLine message board at www.childline.org.uk.

ChildLine
0800 1111

1 *Wie kann man mit ChildLine in Kontakt treten? (4 Wege)*

____

______________________________ (2 P)

2 *Was geschieht, wenn man bei ChildLine anruft?*

____

______________________________ (2 P)

3 *Welche Informationen muss man geben, wenn man bei ChildLine anruft?*

______________________________ (2 P)

1 Adapted from: Bullying ... What can I do? (www.respectme.org.uk/cyberbullying.html)

4 *Was können die Berater tun, um zu helfen? (3 Fakten) Was tun sie nicht? (1 Fakt)*

____

____

____

____ (4 P)

5 *Wie oft kann man bei ChildLine anrufen?*

____ (2 P)

5 REVISION LANGUAGE An interview

You meet a woman who works for ChildLine and ask her six questions about her job and bullying.

a) Choose three verbs from the box and make questions. _____/3

Do …? • Does …? • Are …? • Is …? • Have …? • Has …?

1 ____?

2 ____?

3 ____?

b) Choose three question words from the box and make questions. _____/3

How …? • Why …? • What …? • When …? • Where …?

1 ____?

2 ____?

3 ____?

Klassenarbeit B

Gesamtpunktzahl ______/76 Note ______

1 LISTENING Improving the school climate

Charlie is a reporter for the school radio at Parkside School. He is interviewing teachers and students about the school's project days.

5 **a)** Listen to the first part. Then tick (✓) the correct ending. ____/4

1	The project days were organized ...	because all schools have to have them.	
		to celebrate the good school climate.	
		because the students didn't get on very well.	
		because the school wanted to do something exciting.	
2	The aim of the project days is ...	for students to learn to respect the teachers.	
		to train students to deal with bullying.	
		to make the school a better place.	
		to win a school competition.	
3	Last year, the project days ...	took place at the beginning of summer.	
		were moved to the week before Christmas.	
		took place at the end of autumn.	
		were organized for the new students only.	
4	Mrs Cooper is happy because ...	the school radio wants to inform students about the project days.	
		other schools are interested in learning more about the project days.	
		Charlie had time to interview her.	
		all the students loved the project days.	

6 **b)** Now listen to the second part of the programme. Then tick (✓) right or wrong. ____/4

		right	wrong
1	Brianna liked the first day because they could talk so much.		
2	Brianna preferred the second day.		
3	Brianna thinks that some experiments were too dangerous.		
4	Brianna talks about a student who had a big success.		
5	Brianna thinks that one of the students will do a difficult task the following day.		
6	Brianna thinks that it can be helpful to change roles.		
7	Brianna says that some tasks weren't so good for shyer students.		
8	Brianna suggests having cyberbullying as a topic next year.		

7 **c)** Now listen to the third part and answer the questions.
You don't have to write complete sentences.

_____/4

1 What project did they do in year 8?

____

2 Where did the students in year 8 go during the project days? Give three examples.

____

3 What did Sinan do in his social job? Name three things.

____

4 How, according to Sinan, can working with old people improve the school climate?

____

2 WORDS Understanding new words

Parkside School supports volunteer work during the school year, but also during the holidays. Read Oliver's report for the school website.

VOLUNTEERS, VOLUNTEERS!

Contact

About us

Home

Wow, what a week – tiring, but also very rewarding! I went on a trip to the Lake District with a group of disadvantaged children and their carers. It was my first time volunteering! There were five other volunteers, and our job was to help the carers. Ayla and I were in charge of a group of four primary school kids, who had never been on holiday before. There were outdoor adventure activities, indoor games, lots of sports and plenty of fun. The organization provided everything – tents, sleeping bags, hiking gear, canoes, slack lines, games etc. It was great to see these kids in action! And I think they really benefitted from having a routine and clear rules. They got more and more confident and relaxed every day. If I get the chance, I'd love to volunteer again next summer.

Oliver, year 10

a) Guess the meaning of the following words. They are similar to words that you know. ____/3

tiring: ____________________

disadvantaged: ____________________

relaxed: ____________________

b) Find out the meaning of the other new words. The dictionary entries can help you. ____/7

rewarding: ____________________

carer: ____________________

(to be) in charge of: ____________________

plenty of: ____________________

(to) provide: ____________________

(to) benefit: ____________________

confident: ____________________

reward[1] /rɪ'wɔ:d/ *Substantiv* Belohnung
reward[2] /rɪ'wɔ:d/ *Verb* belohnen
rewarding /rɪ'wɔ:dɪŋ/
1 *allg* lohnend; *finanziell* einträglich
2 (*book etc*) lesenswert (*Buch etc*); (*film etc*) sehenswert (*Film etc*); (*work*) bereichernd, befriedigend (*Arbeit*)

carer /'keərə(r)/ (*BE*) (AE **caregiver**)
1 pflegende(r) Angehörige(r)
2 Betreuer(in): ***Bill is the children's main carer.***

charge[1] /tʃɑ:dʒ/ *Substantiv*
1 ≈ *Kosten* Gebühr: ***It's free of charge.*** Es ist kostenlos.
2 in charge verantwortlich: ***He's in charge of organizing the match.*** Er ist für die Organisation des Spiels verantwortlich.
3 RECHT Anklage
4 MILITÄR Angriff
charge[2] /tʃɑ:dʒ/ *Verb* (***charging***)
1 (*sum of money*) berechnen, verlangen (*Geldsumme*): ***Do they charge for admission?*** Verlangen sie Eintritt?
2 (*customer*) berechnen (*Kunden*)
3 *AE* mit Kreditkarte bezahlen
4 RECHT anklagen: ***She was charged with murder.*** Sie wurde wegen Mordes angeklagt.
5 MILITÄR angreifen
charger /'tʃɑ:dʒə/ *für Batterie, Handy* Ladegerät

plenty[1] /'plenti/ *Pronomen*
1 reichlich
2 plenty of … reichlich …
plenty[2] /'plenti/ *Adverb*
1 plenty more viel mehr
2 plenty big/long/… enough *umg* groß/lang/… genug
plenty[3] /'plenti/ *Substantiv gehoben*
1 Überfluss
2 in plenty in Hülle und Fülle

provide /prə'vaɪd/ (***providing***)
1 *allg* zur Verfügung stellen
2 (*opportunity, service*) bieten (*Gelegenheit, Service*)
3 provide someone with something jemanden mit etwas versorgen
▸ **provide for** /prə'vaɪd fə/
1 provide for someone für jemanden sorgen
2 provide for something auf etwas vorbereitet sein
provided /prə'vaɪdɪd/, **provided that** /prə'vaɪdɪd ðæt/ vorausgesetzt(, dass)
provider /prə'vaɪdə/
1 INTERNET Provider, Anbieter
2 *der Familie usw* Ernährer(in)

benefit[1] /'benɪfɪt/ *Substantiv*
1 *allg* Nutzen, Vorteil
2 *vom Staat* Unterstützung: ***child benefit*** Kindergeld • ***housing benefit*** Wohngeld
3 *vom Arbeitgeber* Leistung
4 *Veranstaltung* Benefizveranstaltung: ***a benefit concert*** ein Benefizkonzert
benefit[2] /'benɪfɪt/ *Verb* (→ *fit*[1])
1 benefit from something von etwas profitieren
2 benefit someone jemandem nützen

confident /'kɒnfɪdənt/
1 *sich seiner sicher* selbstsicher
2 ≈ *zuversichtlich* überzeugt, sicher: ***I am confident that …*** Ich bin davon überzeugt, dass …
confidential /ˌkɒnfɪ'denʃl/ vertraulich

3 LANGUAGE Visitors at Parkside School

____/12

More help p. 61

There are visitors at Parkside School. They are teachers and students from another school and want to learn more about the project days. Write their questions.

Indirekte Rede (Fragen)

Wiederhole kurz die Eckpunkte der indirekten Fragen, bevor du mit der Aufgabe beginnst:
- Wie verändert sich die Zeit?
- Was muss man oft auch noch verändern?
- Wie verändert sich die Satzstellung?
- Wann muss man ein zusätzliches Wort einfügen?

Harry

1 Why do you have project days at your school?

Harry asked us ______________________

____

____

Mr Dixon

2 Do you like the project days?

Mr Dixon asked us ______________________

____

____

Amy

3 Do classes do something different every year?

Amy wanted to know ______________________

____

____

Mrs Smith

4 Are there any new ideas for next year?

Mrs Smith wanted to know ______________________

____

____

Akim

5 How do the projects improve the school climate?

Akim wanted to know ______________________

____

____

Ewa

6 Mrs Cooper, can we come again next year?

Ewa asked Mrs Cooper ______________________

____

____

4 WRITING Giving and getting respect in the city

____/15

More help p. 62

Look at the poster and think of different situations where respect in the city is important. Then write a comment about what respect in the city means to you. Write about 100–120 words.

5 SPEAKING Making small talk

____/15

8

Leila and Luke are in the school canteen. They are talking to each other for the first time. Listen to their conversation.

Now you

João from Portugal is a new student in your class in Germany, but he doesn't speak any German yet. Find a partner (who is João) and talk. The role card on page 27 can help you (the role card for João is on page 18 of your *Lösungsheft*). Make notes first.

Wenn du dich noch unsicher fühlst, kannst du dir in deinem Schülerbuch auf S. 170/171 *(Skills file 7.2: Successful conversations)* Hilfe holen.

Rolecard: You

You start:
- Say hello to the new student.
- Introduce yourself.

Ask your partner some questions, e.g.:
- where he's from
- why he came to Germany
- how he likes it
- if he has been to Germany before
- what he's interested in

React to what your partner says.

Also tell your partner a little bit about yourself, your school, your town, e.g.:
- if you've already been to Portugal
- what you're interested in
- activities you can do at the school
- interesting things to see in your town

End the conversation.

Be polite! Be positive! Be open!

6 MEDIATION An adventure activity day at a German school

____/12

Erlebnispädagogik an der Realschule

HEITERSHEIM. „Wir haben ganz neue Dinge gelernt!" – „Ein Schultag, an den wir uns erinnern werden." – so oder ähnlich waren die Kommentare der Schülerinnen und Schüler der 7. Klassen am Ende des erlebnispädagogischen Vormittags. Für diese Aktion war ein Trainerteam von Experten für Erlebnispädagogik an die Johanniter-Realschule Heitersheim gekommen. Sie hatten im Vorfeld einen Parcours von zwölf unterschiedlichen Stationen für die insgesamt sechs Schülergruppen im großen Schulhof aufgebaut. Das herrliche Herbstwetter unterstützte die Aktionen und machte zusätzlich gute Laune.

Johanniter-Realschule: Mut war beim erlebnispädagogischen Tag gefragt. Foto: U. Peise

Der Parcours, den alle Gruppen durchliefen, förderte ganz unterschiedliche Fertigkeiten. „Die Schüler sollen auch an ihre Grenzen kommen und ganz neue Dinge tun", erläuterte einer der Trainer.

Besonders die Leiterübung, die in den hohen Bäumen stattfand, stellte eine große Herausforderung für jeden Einzelnen dar. „Ich hatte schon Angst vor dem Klettern, als ich die hohe Leiter sah", sagte einer der Schüler. Und genauso ging es fast allen. Wer es aber geschafft hatte, und das waren die meisten, kam überglücklich unten wieder an. Was für eine Erfahrung!

Ganz andere Fertigkeiten waren beim „Robotertanz" gefragt. Hier wurde ein „blinder" Partner über die Tanzfläche geführt – gesprochen wurde dabei kein Wort, denn die Richtung wurde jeweils durch bestimmte Körperbewegungen übermittelt.

Der vom Freundeskreis der Schule gesponserte Vormittag war nicht nur in den Augen der drei siebten Klassen ein voller Erfolg. Der Schulleiter sowie die Klassenlehrer waren voll zufrieden und überlegen nun, solche Tage regelmäßig durchzuführen.

João saw this article about your school and wants to know what it is about.
Tell him about the most important facts in English:

- the topic of the day (1 P)
- who it was for (1 P)
- who organized it (1 P)
- what the students did (give examples) (3 P)
- how the students felt (2 P)
- what students, teachers and the principal think about it (2 P)
- plans for the future (2 P)

Klassenarbeit A

Gesamtpunktzahl ______/61 Note ______

1 READING Tips for job interviews

My School | Interview with Alan Green | Info | Contact

Alan Green

At this time of the year many students are looking for jobs. Even if you are very confident, a job interview can make you feel nervous. As we want you to be successful, we talked to Alan Green, the manager of AAO, a big company in our area, and asked him to give us some tips. This is what we talked about. Good luck, everybody! *Sarah and Alfie*

Ⓐ

Good afternoon, Mr Green! Thanks for taking the time to talk to us.

You're welcome. I'm happy to help.

These days we, like many other students, are looking for jobs or the chance to get some work experience. This means that we are facing our first job interviews. You kindly agreed to give us some tips on how to prepare for an interview.

Yes, I think it's very important to talk about this because job interviews make people feel nervous, no matter how confident they are. And the only thing you can do is prepare.

Ⓑ

So, according to you, what can candidates do to be well-prepared for an interview?

A good and intensive preparation will help a lot of people to feel calmer. First of all, do some research. For example:

- Check the company's website and get as much information as you can.
- Maybe you even know someone who works there. Talk to them and find out what they do and what the company is like.
- Read the job advert carefully. Find out what skills and strengths are needed. It's important to match your strengths with the skills asked for in the job advert.

So during the interview, should candidates say or show that they've checked the website?

Absolutely, yes. This can be very helpful. You should be able to say more about the website, though. Don't just say 'Oh, I found your website very interesting.' Say what you found very interesting, and why.

Ⓒ

Ⓓ

OK, let's get back to the strengths – they are important, aren't they?

Yes, definitely. You should know your strengths. Keep in mind that there are lots of other candidates for the job. So when you prepare for the interview, think about your strengths – what makes you stand out? Why should the company choose you instead of someone else? Think of some examples: in what situations, at school or somewhere else, did you use your strengths to fix a problem?

So we should give examples again?

That's it, yes. You should always be able to go into detail, so think about lots of examples when you get ready for the interview. Be prepared to talk about relevant work at school, your achievements in other jobs or about volunteer work that you've done.

This sounds like a lot of talk about how great you are. What's your advice for candidates who aren't that confident?

My advice is: be honest and don't lie. Simply be yourself. The interviewer will notice if you're pretending to be someone else. This is important for everybody, though, not just for shy candidates. (E)

An important issue for students is clothes. What do you suggest students should wear to an interview? (F)

No matter what you're wearing – your clothes have to be clean. And they should be suitable for the job you're applying for.
This reminds me of another important point: be punctual. Try to be there fifteen minutes before the interview starts. This gives you time to check your appearance, drink a glass of water, go through your notes again – things like that.

That's a good tip. And it sounds easy to follow. (G)

Yes, it's simple and very effective. My advice for you is this: a few days before the interview, check how to get to the company and find out how long it takes to get there. This will help you feel even calmer.

Do you have any other tips? Maybe something we haven't talked about yet? (H)

Let me think ... Yes. Most interviewers will give you the chance to ask questions when they have finished questioning you. This is your chance to show that you're really interested in the job – ask questions about the company, the job, and the team. It's usually your last chance to show that you're keen on working with them.

Thank you! Those were some really helpful tips. Now it's up to us to follow them.

Thank you, too, and good luck to all of you!

a) Read the interview. In which of the eight paragraphs A–H do you find which information? Sometimes you find the information in more than one paragraph. ____/8

	In which paragraph of the interview do you learn ...	Paragraph(s):	
1	... what's important on the day of the interview?		(1 P)
2	... how to prepare for the interview?		(3 P)
3	... what to do at the end of the interview?		(1 P)
4	... what to say or not to say during the interview?		(2 P)
5	... why Alfie and Sarah are interviewing Mr Green?		(1 P)

b) Read the interview again and complete the sentences with information from the text. ____/8

Sätze vervollständigen

Achte darauf, dass dein fertiger Satz sowohl inhaltlich als auch grammatikalisch korrekt ist. Meist gibt es nicht nur eine richtige Lösung – es sind viele verschiedene Formulierungen für einen inhaltlichen Aspekt möglich.

1 Sarah and Alfie talk to Mr Green because many students at their school ______________________

____. (1P)

2 There are two ways to find out more about the company:

– ____. (1 P)

– ____. (1 P)

3 When you talk about the website during the interview, ______________________

____. (1 P)

4 During the interview, it's important to show how your strengths ______________________

____. (1 P)

5 To make sure that you are on time for the interview, you should ______________________

______________________ a few days before the interview and ______________________

______________________ on the day of the interview. (2 P)

6 At the end of the interview, don't just get up and leave, but ______________________

____. (1 P)

2 WORDS Words that form groups

____/12

Look at the words in the box. Make four groups with four words each. Then choose a topic from the box for each group. There are more words than you need.

More help p. 64

admire • application • assistant • ~~earn~~ • cover letter • confident • necessary • reporter • application form • working hours • qualities • CV • stylist • ~~run out of money~~ • hotel manager • jobs • ~~getting on with money~~ • information about work • ~~budget~~ • energetic • pay • boardwalk • shift • enthusiastic • reference • reliable • breaks • ~~overspend~~

words	topic
› *earn, budget, overspend, run out of money*	› *getting on with money*

3 LANGUAGE Questions for the interview

You're preparing for a job interview. Choose one of the job ads below and think of six questions that you could ask at the end of the interview. You can ask about the working hours, the date for a decision, the team, your first day, your jobs, any special clothes, etc.

____/6

☞ Wiederhole vor Beginn der Aufgabe noch einmal die Wortstellung in Fragen (*Language file 12* auf S. 189 in deinem Schülerbuch).

The Lakeside Cafe ...

... is looking for a **cook's assistant**

to support the team **during the summer**.

No experience needed.

Just come inside and ask for Sheila.

TOM'S GARAGE

WANTED:

car mechanic

or helping hand.

Must be reliable.

For more information call

Tom Jones at 029 1234567.

Join our team!

We're looking for

a flexible stylist.

Ask inside.

Sunny Hairdresser's

Do you enjoy working with children? Are you experienced and patient?

Apply for a job as a kindergarten teacher at Forest Hill Kindergarten.

info@forest-hill-kids.co.uk

1 ____?

2 ____?

3 ____?

4 ____?

5 ____?

6 ____?

4 WRITING An application letter

Look at the job advert and write an application letter. Write 120–180 words.

____/15

More help p. 64/65

Down Under wants you

Looking for a six-month job in Australia? This is your chance!

Why not get some international experience before you start a job in your home country?

Australia City Jobs is looking for students from all over the world to work here in Australia. We have lots of different jobs waiting for you. You'll be working in one of our hotels or restaurants in one of Australia's great cities.

For example, you could be helping in the kitchen or the outdoor area, cleaning the guest rooms, working as receptionist or waiter/waitress.

What we offer you:

! 30 hours of work per week
! one or two days off every week
! good pocket money
! free accommodation and food

Write a letter of application to ACJ with details about:

! the job you're applying for
! your qualifications
! your past work experience
! the best time for you to start working
! your favourite place in Australia

Don't miss your chance! Get to know Down Under and work here at the same time!

The Manager | ACJ | Manchester Street | Sydney

You can start like this:

Dear ____________________

5 SPEAKING Training for job interviews

You've found a website that helps candidates prepare for job interviews. It also offers typical interview questions that you can listen to and answer.

9 **a)** Read the interview questions and make notes. Then put away your notes, listen to the first part and answer the questions. ____/7

- Hör zu und sprich erst, wenn du den Piepton hörst.
- Du kannst die Aufnahme unterbrechen, wenn du mehr Zeit benötigst.
- Sei höflich und antworte in ganzen Sätzen.
- Du kannst dich selbst auch aufnehmen und die Übung öfter machen.

Manager Hello, and welcome. Please sit down and make yourself comfortable. Did you find our offices right away?

You ______

Manager Ok, today we want to find out more about you and your skills and work experience. In this job you will need to work with the computer a lot. Tell me, what IT skills do you have?

You ______

Manager Can you tell me about your strengths?

You ____

____

Manager That sounds interesting. What about talking in front of people? Is this something you're comfortable with?

You ____

____

Manager Can you give me an example?

You ____

____

Manager How do you think that someone who knows you well would describe you?

You ____

____

Manager Sometimes you have to fix problems. Which of your strengths do you think will help you to do this?

You ____

____

10 **b)** Now listen to the second part and answer the manager's next questions carefully. Take your time. ____/5

Klassenarbeit B

Gesamtpunktzahl ______/74 Note ______

1 LISTENING Work experience

The students in year 9 at Parkside School have just done a week of work experience. Now they are talking about it in class with their teacher, Mr Conkin.

11 **a)** Listen to the first part and complete the sentences with 1 to 8 words. ____/8

Achte bei *Listening*-Aufgaben immer darauf, dass du dir vor dem ersten Hören die Aufgabe genau anschaust, damit du weißt, worauf du beim Hören besonders achten musst. Im Fall dieser Aufgabe solltest du auch die Satzanfänge vorher lesen.

1 Mr Conkin asks the students to tell the class about ______________________ ______________________.

2 Sophie worked at the City Council because ______________________ ______________________.

3 At the beginning it was boring because ______________________ ______________________.

4 The City Council wanted to find out about how ______________________ feel, what they need, what they like and ______________________.

5 At first, interviewing people on the street was ______________________ for Sophie because ______________________.

6 But after some interviews, Sophie got ______________________.

7 Sophie found out that she is good at ______________________.

8 Sophie didn't like the ______________________ and the ______________________.

Klassenarbeit A Lösungen

Hinweis Bewertung bei offenen Aufgaben

- Bei manchen Aufgaben gibt es verschiedene Lösungsmöglichkeiten, die im Lösungsheft durch einen Schrägstrich (/) voneinander getrennt werden. Für den Punkt benötigst du nur eine dieser Möglichkeiten. Ausnahme: In der Aufgabenstellung werden zwei oder mehr Lösungen gefordert.
- Eingeklammerte Lösungen sind möglich, aber nicht verpflichtend.

1 READING A window on my life

a) *Lösungsvorschlag:* (12 P)

1 (2 P für einen der beiden folgenden Gründe:)

– Because he was / used to be a student at their school.

– Because he has made his dream come true. / Because he has an interesting job. / Because he's a professional photographer. / ...

2 Because he wasn't sure if he would make enough money. / Because he wanted to have a safe job. / ... (2 P)

3 (2 P für einen der beiden folgenden Fakten:)

– His friends and family ordered/bought copies (as presents) for their friends.

– A calendar business offered him a project. / He got an offer for a photo project from a calendar business. / A calendar business offered him a photo project about Sydney. / ...

4 (je 2 P für zwei verschiedene der folgenden Fakten:)

– He won a photo competition.

– He won a photo camera that allowed him to take better quality photos.

– One of his photos was successful / was a success on the internet. / He sold photos on the internet.

– He sent his calendars to different / many / a few calendar businesses.

– He was offered a photo project by a calendar business. / He got an offer for a photo project from a calendar business. / A calendar business offered him a photo project about Sydney. / ...

5 To learn how to manage/run a business. (2 P)

b) (6 P)

Ⓐ Why I became a photographer / About me / My life as a student at South Sydney High

Ⓑ First steps / Favourite places in Sydney / Why I won the competition

Ⓒ My parents say "no" / My job at the bank / A difficult decision

Ⓓ Successful calendars / Nice friends / Living on very little money

Ⓔ My trip to Bali / Millions of photos! / First job as a photographer

Ⓕ How to run a business / Making a dream come true / Working two jobs

2 WORDS In English, please! (6 P)

1 It's likely to rain.

2 Nothing compares with/to my old bike.

3 The nearest supermarket is in Murray Street.

4 The new film/movie is worth watching. / It's worth watching the new film/movie.

5 We meet regularly every Friday afternoon.

6 Hamid doesn't use his car at all.

3 WORDS Corresponding nouns

a) *Lösungsvorschlag:* (0,5 P für jedes Wortpaar, max. 2 P)

verb/noun	verb/noun	verb/noun	verb/noun
answer	drink	must	sleep
ban	drive	name	smile
beat	email	notice	sound
bite	end	order	spot
book	experience	pass	start
boycott	experiment	phone	stay
break	fall	plan	sting
camp	farm	play	stop
care	fight	practice	structure
change	film	present	surprise
chat	fine	race	talk
check	group	rain	text
comment	hand	rap	train
cook	help	report	turn
copy	hope	respect	visit
cross	interview	ride	volunteer
cruise	joke	risk	walk
dance	land	shout	wave
dream	list	show	work
dress	love	sign	…

b) *Lösungsvorschlag:* (1 P für jedes Wortpaar, max. 4 P)

adjective	noun ending in *-ness*
clever	cleverness
dark	darkness
fit	fitness
friendly	friendliness
happy	happiness
ill	illness
red	redness
sad	sadness

c) (0,5 P pro Wort)

adjective	noun
careful	care
central	centre
hot	heat
traditional	tradition

Lerntipp

Wenn du beim Wörterlernen die dazugehörigen Wörter aus der Wortfamilie gleich mitlernst, festigst du deinen Wortschatz bzw. vergrößerst ihn sogar. Lege dir dazu eine Tabelle mit Wortfamilien an und erweitere sie ständig.

verb	noun	adjective
race	race	
protect	protection	
bleed	blood	
care	care	careful
	fitness	fit

4 LANGUAGE A blog entry from Australia

Hi guys, here we are again!

On our tour through Australia we do/did something special every day, well, nearly every day!

On Monday we arrived here in Sydney and in the afternoon we didn't do anything but sleep. But yesterday was different. As you know, we love adventures, and so we decided not to go on one of those commercial sightseeing tours. Instead, we wanted to explore the city on our own and on foot. So yesterday evening our feet hurt quite a bit, but we were full of exciting impressions of this amazing city. Just have a look at our photos!

At the moment we're having some sandwiches in Hyde Park. Sightseeing makes you hungry!

We don't go to a restaurant every day – it's too expensive. Later we're going to visit the 309 m high Sydney Tower Eye, and we're looking forward to the great view. We're going to post some photos from up there in the next days.

5 MEDIATION Dangers at the beach

Lösungsvorschlag:

Frau Koch	*Wir sind erst gestern angekommen und haben ein paar Fragen. Gibt es irgendwelche Sicherheitsvorschriften, die wir am Strand beachten müssen?*
Du	They arrived yesterday and have a few questions. Are there any safety rules that they have to follow at the beach? (2 P)
Chloe	Well, the sea at some of the most famous beaches can be very dangerous. But there are lifeguards at these beaches, so you should always stay near them. Also you should watch the flags: always swim in the area between the red and the yellow flags. That's the safest area.
Du	*Also, das Meer kann an den meisten berühmten Stränden sehr gefährlich sein. Aber an diesen Stränden gibt es Rettungsschwimmer, also sollten Sie immer in deren Nähe bleiben. Außerdem sollten Sie die Flaggen beachten und immer zwischen der roten und der gelben Flagge schwimmen. Das ist die sicherste Zone.* (3 P)
Frau Koch	*Und wie ist es mit den Haien? Wir haben schon etwas Angst vor Haiangriffen.*
Du	What about sharks? They're a bit afraid of shark attacks. (1 P)
Chloe	Again you should only swim at beaches with lifeguards. Never swim in the dark, or in the early morning. Don't swim too far out into the sea and don't swim near rivers.
Du	*Auch hier gilt: Sie sollten nur an Stränden mit Rettungsschwimmern schwimmen.*

Schwimmen Sie nicht im Dunkeln oder am frühen Morgen. Schwimmen Sie nicht zu weit raus und schwimmen Sie nicht in der Nähe von Flüssen. (2 P)

Herr Koch *Was müssen wir noch beachten?*

Du What else should they keep in mind? (1 P)

Chloe The sun is very strong in Australia. So always protect your skin with strong sun-cream, wear a hat and long shirts. You shouldn't stay out in the sun the whole day.

Du *Die Sonne in Australien ist sehr intensiv. Sie müssen Ihre Haut immer mit starker Sonnencreme schützen, einen Hut und langärmelige T-Shirts tragen. Sie sollten auch nicht den ganzen Tag in der Sonne bleiben.* (2 P)

Frau Koch *Puh, da muss man schon auf einiges aufpassen. Aber ich danke euch beiden ganz herzlich für eure Hilfe.*

Du *Bitte, gern geschehen.* Thanks for your help, Chloe.

6 SPEAKING Your 'Bundesland' – a place to visit?

1 *Lösungsvorschlag:*

Today I want to talk about my 'Bundesland', Berlin. It's special because not only is it a 'Bundesland', but Berlin is also the capital of Germany. It's the biggest city in Germany and a popular place for tourists from all over the world. Let me tell you why.

To begin with, Berlin is a multi-cultural city with a population of 3.5 million. Here you can find people from all different parts of Germany and from all over the world. I love that my city is so international! Because of this, there are also many different kinds of restaurants and cultural events during the year, like the Carnival of Cultures and the Berlinale Film Festival. The atmosphere in Berlin is pretty relaxed, but also very exciting, especially at night!

Next, I'd like to talk about the summer in Berlin. Winter can be very cold, dark and long, but summer is my favourite time of year because it's hot and the sun stays out until 10 pm! This is great because there are many parks where you can go with your friends to relax or to have a barbecue! And if you like swimming, there are many lakes around the city where you can go, such as Wannsee.

Finally, Berlin has a very long and interesting history and many museums where you can learn about the past. My favourite is the East Side Gallery. It's a part of the Berlin Wall that is like one big piece of art and you can visit it for free.

I hope that now you can see why Berlin is a great place for both Berliners and visitors. Thank you for listening.

Klassenarbeit B Lösungen

1 LISTENING Winter in Australia

a) The programme informs about winter in Australia. (1 P)

Hörtext:
2
Part 1

Brad Hello and welcome again! It's the 25th of August and you're listening to Radio Two Oh Two Australia. I'm Brad and today we're going to talk about snow – yes, snow! The news went around the world quickly, so I guess you all know that it snowed in Canberra yesterday – for the first time since 2006. People in Canberra were so excited and posted many different snow pictures on social media. A snowball fight in the garden – for some kids it was the first in their lives! Or a kangaroo in the snow – can you imagine? Or people warming themselves around the barbecue because their houses are too cold. Yes, you heard that correctly – some fires even got out of control, so the fire fighters were very very busy! But the snow didn't come as a surprise because the weather forecast had announced it. So people were actually waiting for the snow to fall.
It started snowing in the early afternoon, so most people were able to watch the snow fall. Because of the ice and snow some roads in Canberra had to be closed for safety reasons, but are open again today.
So today we'd like to talk to Ruby from Victoria. Ruby is an expert on snow in Australia. G'day Ruby, we're happy to have you here in the studio with us. Ruby, Australia and snow – those are two things that couldn't be more different. I mean Australia is known for its sun and deserts. What about snow then?

Ruby You're right, Australia is widely known as a sunshine and beach country, and not as a country that has snow or even a skiing season. Let me give you some details: the regions where it's most likely to snow stretch from New South Wales into Victoria and the Australian Capital Territory – a region known as the *Australian Alps*. The snow here is often one metre high, sometimes more. And the snow is likely to fall from June to September. Snow is possible in other regions too, like South and Western Australia or Queensland, but in those places it's more of a sensation.

Brad Thanks, Ruby, for the information. We'll be right back after some music.

Part 2

Brad Hello, here we are again with our report on snow in Australia. Let's talk about the climate in the Australian Alps, Ruby. Why does it snow only there?

Ruby There are two main reasons why Australia doesn't get much snow. First, Australia is pretty close to the equator, and second, Australia is quite flat. So 75 % of Australia's land area is flat, hot desert. Now the Australian Alps are different in two ways: they are closer to Antarctica than the rest of Australia, and, in the mountains, the higher you go, the colder it gets. So in June, at the beginning of winter, heavy storms from the southern ocean hit the mountains and push the temperatures below zero. And some of the mountains are very high. Mount Kosciuszko, Australia's highest mountain, is 2228 metres high. That's why the Australian Alps are almost the only region that gets snow every year.

Brad You explained that very well. Thanks, Ruby. So what can you tell us about winter sport and skiing in the Australian Alps?

Ruby Winter sports have become very popular in the last years, so more and more places in the Australian Alps have become skiing spots. You can find ski schools everywhere! By the way, did you know how skiing came to Australia?

Brad	No, tell us!
Ruby	Well, back in 1861 people from Northern Europe came to Australia to look for gold in New South Wales. They started the first skiing club in Kiandra. But it took many more years to make skiing and snowboarding popular in Australia and today – more than 150 years later – there are quite a few tourist hot spots in the Australian Alps.
Brad	That's interesting. So what do you think people enjoy the most in the ski regions?
Ruby	Hmm, it's difficult to say. Skiing and snowboarding are THE most popular sports during the winter months, a great change to the usual summer sports. Another thing is the beautiful winter landscape, you know, people aren't used to snow-covered mountains, so they are a great attraction for Australians.
Brad	Yes, I'm sure they are, and I'll definitely be the next visitor in the Australian Alps. So thank you very much for sharing, Ruby. If you, our listeners, have any more questions about skiing, snowboarding or simply visiting the Australian Alps, you can ask Ruby. After some music we'll be right back.

3 **b)** *Hörtext:* (part 1 again)

1	In Canberra ...	it snows very often.	
		it hasn't snowed for many years.	✓
		it has never snowed before.	
2	People in Canberra ...	sent round the news quickly.	✓
		don't like the snow.	
		were surprised about the snow.	
3	There were problems in Canberra because ...	snowball fights got out of control.	
		some kangaroos died in the cold.	
		there were dangerous fires.	✓
4	The snow in Canberra ...	started during the day.	✓
		wasn't dangerous for traffic.	
		stopped after an hour.	
5	The snow ...	makes it possible to go skiing.	✓
		usually falls in December.	
		is likely to fall in the desert.	

4 **c)** *Hörtext:* (part 2 again)

		right	wrong
1	It snows in the Australian Alps because they are higher than the rest of the country.	✓	
2	In June, temperatures in the Australian Alps go up.		✓
3	The highest mountain is more than 2000 metres high.	✓	
4	Australians don't like winter sports so much.		✓
5	Skiing came to Australia about 150 years ago.	✓	
6	Australian kids learn how to ski and snowboard in high school.		✓
7	Australians don't enjoy the snow because they aren't used to it.		✓

2 WORDS A crossword

Across

2 In Australia you should always protect your head from the sun.

4 Ruby knows very much about the Australian Alps. She's an expert on them.

7 Some people call me 'Shorty', but I don't like that nickname very much.

9 Australia is the smallest of the seven continents.

10 Little kids shouldn't stay in the sun too much. It's better for them to play in the shade.

Down

1 I bought a waterproof watch because I often go swimming.

3 A person who is from Australia is an Australian citizen.

5 This book is great! I'll continue to read it at home.

6 The bite of a dangerous spider can be deadly.

8 If a boat gets into bad weather it's important to have a good crew on board.

3 WORDS Opposites and synonyms

a)

1	narrow	≠	wide (1 P)
2	(to) die	≠	(to) be born (1 P)
3	(the) cold	≠	(the) heat (1 P)

b)

1	nearly	=	almost (1 P)
2	(to) go on	=	(to) continue (1 P)
3	(to) repair a bike	=	(to) fix a bike (1 P)

4 LANGUAGE About my classmates

Lösungsvorschlag:

1 visit Australia soon: Cem is going to visit Australia soon. / Cem isn't going to visit Australia soon. / Cem will visit Australia soon. / Cem won't visit Australia soon. (1 P)

2 try kangaroo meat: Lina has tried kangaroo meat. / Lina hasn't tried kangaroo meat. (1 P)

3 give a talk about Australia last month: Max gave a talk about Australia last month. / Max didn't give a talk about Australia last month. (1 P)

4 be born in Australia: Daniel was born in Australia. / Daniel wasn't born in Australia. (1 P)

5 know a lot about the First Australians: Nele knows a lot about the First Australians. / Nele doesn't know a lot about the First Australians. (1 P)

6 read a book about Australia at the moment: Paul is reading a book about Australia at the moment. / Paul isn't reading a book about Australia at the moment. (1 P)

7 be afraid of sharks: Nesrin is afraid of sharks. / Nesrin isn't afraid of sharks. (1 P)

5 REVISION LANGUAGE An interview (6 P)

Auswahl möglicher Fragen:

1 Do you like winter? (simple present)
2 Which are the winter months in Australia? (simple present)
3 How long is the Australian winter? (simple present)
4 How cold does it get in winter? (simple present)
5 When was the last time it snowed? (simple past)
6 Will you go skiing in the winter? (will-future)
7 Have you ever seen snow in Australia? (present perfect)
8 Do Australian people like snow? (simple present)
9 Do many Australian people go skiing or snowboarding? (simple present)
10 Can you ski? (simple present)
11 Where are the hot spots for skiing in Australia? (simple present)
12 What do you prefer: winter or summer? (simple present)

6 WRITING Jill's day in the snow (15 P)

Lösungsvorschlag:

Last Tuesday the weather forecast announced snow for Wednesday, so I was very excited. But when I looked out of the window on Wednesday morning I was a bit disappointed because there wasn't any snow.

During the geography lesson it finally started to snow. All the students ran to the windows to watch it. After school we met to play out in the snow. Of course we all took lots of photos and sent them to our friends around the world. In the evening our house was so cold we had to warm ourselves around the barbecue. The next morning the snow was all gone. I'm happy that I have lots of photos so I can remember this exciting day in Canberra.

Klassenarbeit A Lösungen

1 READING Dealing with your feelings

a) The text is about how to deal with bullying. (1 P)

b) (14 P)

		right	wrong	not in the text
1	Everybody has a good strategy against bullying.		✓	
2	Having positive things in your life can help a lot.	✓		
3	Everybody should get at least one compliment a day.			✓
4	If you respect others, they will respect you.			✓
5	Every student should learn about bullying at school.			✓
6	You can fight bullying easily if you know how.		✓	
7	Ignoring the problem is a good way of taking control of your life.		✓	
8	There are different ways of dealing with bullying.	✓		
9	You should look out for healthy ways to get on with the problem.	✓		
10	Staying at home a lot will make you feel better.		✓	
11	It's good to find someone you can talk to.	✓		
12	The internet is not a good place for help.		✓	
13	Think about your hobbies and find people with the same hobbies.	✓		
14	Going to a club once a week can make you feel better.			✓

2 WORDS Say it in English

1 This is such a great shop. (1 P)

2 Your opinion matters. / Your opinion is important. (1 P)

3 Don't be a pain. (1 P)

4 I have every right to be here. / It's my right to be here. (1 P)

5 By the way, I got a role in the school play. (1 P)

6 I warned him not to go there. / I warned him about going there. (1 P)

7 I haven't seen Paula lately. (1 P)

8 We don't agree on everything. (1 P)

3 LANGUAGE A class discussion about bullying

a)

1 Katie said that some of her classmates called her names. (1,5 P)

2 Ethan complained that Jack and Igor made fun of him. (1,5 P)

3 Molly said that Jessica sometimes kicked her. (1,5 P)

4 Omar said/complained/... that he got mean text messages again and again. (1,5 P)

Lerntipp	Indirekte Rede (Aussagesätze und Fragen)
So kannst du einen Aussage- oder Fragesatz in die indirekte Rede setzen:	
Aussage	
direkt	Emily: **I** **live** with **my** grandparents.
indirekt	Emily **said** that **she lived** with **her** grandparents.
Frage	
direkt	Emily: Do **you** **like** sports, Hassan?
indirekt	Emily **asked** Hassan **if** **he** **liked** sports.

b)

1 The teacher asked them / the kids / the bullies / us not to call Katie names. (1,5 P)

2 She told them / Jack and Igor to stop making fun of Ethan / not to make fun of Ethan (anymore). (1,5 P)

3 She told her/Jessica not to kick Molly again. (1,5 P)

4 She told them / the kids / the bullies / us not to write mean text messages and to do their/our homework instead. (1,5 P)

Lerntipp	Indirekte Rede (Aufforderungen, Bitten, Ratschläge)
So kannst du Aufforderungen, Bitten und Ratschläge in die indirekte Rede setzen:	
direkt	Emily: Simon, **look** at **me**. **Don't be** shy!
indirekt	Emily **told** Simon **to look** at **her** and **not to be** shy.

4 MEDIATION About ChildLine

Lösungsvorschlag:

Hinweis

Bei allen Fragen sind sowohl Formulierungen mit „man/einem/einen" (Bsp.: Man wird mit jemandem verbunden, der einem zuhört.) als auch mit „du/dir/dich" (Bsp.: Du wirst mit jemandem verbunden, der dir zuhört.) in Ordnung.

1 Kontaktmöglichkeiten:

- anrufen (0,5 P)
- E-Mail schicken (0,5 P)
- online mit einem Berater chatten (0,5 P)
- Nachricht auf dem *message board* der Homepage hinterlassen (0,5 P)

2 Man wird mit jemandem verbunden, der einem zuhört. / Man kann mit jemandem über das Problem sprechen. / Man wird mit einem Berater verbunden. / … (2 P)

3 Man muss keine Informationen geben. / Man muss weder den Namen noch andere Details angeben. / Man muss keine Fragen beantworten. / … (2 P)

4 Was können die Berater für einen tun? (je 1 P für drei verschiedene der folgenden Dinge:)

- Sie hören zu.
- Sie stellen Fragen.
- Sie versuchen zu verstehen, wie es dir geht.
- Sie helfen dir zu überlegen / Sie beraten mit dir, was du in deinem Leben ändern solltest und wer dich dabei unterstützen könnte.

Was tun die Berater nicht?

Sie verurteilen dich nicht. / Sie sagen dir nicht, was richtig oder falsch ist. (1 P)

5 Sooft man will. / Man kann sich immer wieder melden, sogar, wenn man beim ersten Mal nichts erzählt hat. (2 P)

5 REVISION LANGUAGE An interview

Lösungsvorschlag:

a)

- **Do** you like your job? / **Do** you have children too? / …
- **Doesn't** it make you sad to listen to problems all the time? / **Does** age make a difference? / …
- **Are** there differences between girls and boys? / **Are** some children more likely to get bullied than others? / …
- **Isn't** your job sometimes hard? / **Is** it a good idea to talk to a teacher if you get bullied? / …
- **Have** you ever met one of the kids that called you? / **Have** you ever been bullied yourself? / …
- **Has** bullying changed over the years? / **Has** bullying always been such a big problem? / …

b)

- **How** old are most of the kids when they call you? / **How** do younger kids deal with bullying? / …
- **Why** do you think some kids become bullies? / **Why** did you want to work at ChildLine? / …
- **What** can kids do against bullies? / **What's** the difference between bullying and a normal fight? / …
- **When** did you start working for ChildLine? / **When** should parents or teachers call the police? / …
- **Where** does most of the bullying happen? / **Where** can parents get information if their child gets bullied? / …

Klassenarbeit B Lösungen

1 LISTENING Improving the school climate

a) *Hörtext:*

5

Charlie Hello everybody, this is Parkside School Radio, and I'm Charlie. Welcome to today's programme. Today we're talking about project days at our school. This week we have project days and everybody is super excited. But what is it all about? To find out, we're going to talk to several people. Our first person on the programme today: head teacher Mrs Cooper.

Mrs Cooper Come in! Oh hello, Charlie!

Charlie Hello, Mrs Cooper, how are you doing?

Mrs Cooper Not bad. What can I do to help you?

Charlie We're doing a programme for the school radio about project days and I was wondering, could you give us some time for a quick interview?

Mrs Cooper Yes, I can. What would you like to know?

Charlie Well, as you know project days is very popular here at school and everybody is super excited. Maybe you can tell us: how did it all start?

Mrs Cooper Well, about five years ago there was a lot of bullying at this school, aggressive behaviour, students calling each other names, fighting and so on. So the school decided to improve the school climate and introduced the project days.

Charlie Ah, ok. So in your opinion: how did the project days help?

Mrs Cooper Well, students get to know each other outside the usual classroom context. Students from all different backgrounds learn how to respect each other. And it also creates a very positive atmosphere for the students. And thus the students can, well, learn better.

Charlie And in the past project days used to take place in June, so more toward the end of the year. This year it's much earlier. Why is that?

Mrs Cooper Well, we decided that it's better to have the project days at the beginning of the school year because of the new students. So the school decided to move the project days to the beginning of autumn.

Charlie Alright, I understand. Well, that sounds like a very good idea. It creates a good atmosphere right from the start. Is there anything else you'd like to say about the project days?

Mrs Cooper Only that I'm very happy and proud to say that the project days have been such a success. So much so that we've had teachers and students from other schools coming here to find out what it's all about.

Charlie Wow, great! Well, I think that's all for now. Thanks for the information and of course for your time, Mrs Cooper. Have a great day!

Mrs Cooper Yes, you too! Bye bye, Charlie!

Charlie Bye, take care!

1	The project days were organized ...	because all schools have to have them.	
		to celebrate the good school climate.	
		because the students didn't get on very well.	✓
		because the school wanted to do something exciting.	
2	The aim of the project days is ...	for students to learn to respect the teachers.	
		to train students to deal with bullying.	
		to make the school a better place.	✓
		to win a school competition.	
3	Last year, the project days ...	took place at the beginning of summer.	✓
		were moved to the week before Christmas.	
		took place at the end of autumn.	
		were organized for the new students only.	
4	Mrs Cooper is happy because ...	the school radio wants to inform students about the project days.	
		other schools are interested in learning more about the project days.	✓
		Charlie had time to interview her.	
		all the students loved the project days.	

b) *Hörtext:*

6

Charlie Oh, hi there, Brianna, can I just stop you for a minute? As you might know we're doing ... for the radio programme, we're doing a few interviews for project days, to ask students and teachers, you know, what they think of it, and how they like it. Can I just interview you for a minute?

Brianna Sure, yeah. What would you like to know?

Charlie Maybe you can tell us your name again, the class you're in and your age.

Brianna Ok. Well, my name is Brianna, I'm in year 7 and I'm twelve years old.

Charlie Alright. And maybe you can tell us about your project in year 7.

Brianna Well, the topic that we got was "Trusting each other". It was really, really interesting. So the first day though, there was a lot of talking because we all had a lot to say. Really, after a while it was a bit too much. But the second day, that was the best because on that day we were doing experiments and ... sort of doing things where we could learn how to trust each other.

Charlie Like, for example? What do you mean?

Brianna Well, doing really difficult tasks in a team. Like ... one thing we had to do – this was really hard – was we had to cover our eyes for three hours ...

Charlie Oh wow!

Brianna Yeah ... and our partner had to steer us round and make sure that we didn't crash. Some of the things we did, they were actually even a bit dangerous. So some of the students didn't want to do them at first, like one of the things was we had to jump into the arms of our classmates and hope they'd catch us.

Charlie Wow, tell me more about that. That sounds really interesting.

Brianna Yeah, there was ... well, there was one girl actually who – she didn't want to do it at first, but she did in the end and she was really proud and happy when she did it and all of us were cheering her on. But there was one boy – he hasn't done his jump yet, but he wants to try again tomorrow and I think he'll do it and we'll be there for him.

Charlie And what would you say, what do you think the students have learned so far from the experience?

Brianna Well, it's been really great just as a way to get to know each other better because you ended up having to be paired with people who weren't maybe your normal friends who you hung out with. And it was also one thing which was really interesting about the experiments was it meant that you – sometimes you had to change roles, so like maybe people ... when you were blind, people who normally would be really confident, they were in a really weak role and having to trust someone else. So that was I think a really good experience ... Yeah, and I was just gonna say that also for some of the shyer students – I'm quite confident – but some of the shyer ones, you know, it gave them the opportunity to be the leader and be able to sort of take ... be empowered that way. So it was great!

Charlie So from everything you're saying ... it sounds like you liked it a lot so far. Is that right?

Brianna Yeah, it was great! I mean the only thing I would say ... the only bad thing was that there wasn't enough time. I think that project days should be longer and there should maybe even be a second week during or at the end of the school year or something.

Charlie So maybe any tips or ideas for next year?

Brianna I think what would be really cool would be if we could do a project about social media. Because that's, you know, really relevant to everyone, so that would be super.

Charlie Yeah, that does sound like a good idea. Alright, well thanks a lot, Brianna, thanks for your time and, well, have a great day!

Brianna Thank you!

Charlie Bye now!

Brianna Bye!

		right	wrong
1	Brianna liked the first day because they could talk so much. (0,5 P)		✓
2	Brianna preferred the second day. (0,5 P)	✓	
3	Brianna thinks that some experiments were too dangerous. (0,5 P)		✓
4	Brianna talks about a student who had a big success. (0,5 P)	✓	
5	Brianna thinks that one of the students will do a difficult task the following day. (0,5 P)	✓	
6	Brianna thinks that it can be helpful to change roles. (0,5 P)	✓	
7	Brianna says that some tasks weren't so good for shyer students. (0,5 P)		✓
8	Brianna suggests having cyberbullying as a topic next year. (0,5 P)		✓

c) *Hörtext:*

7

Charlie Hey, that looks like Sinan. Hey, Sinan, can I talk to you for just a second?

Sinan Yeah. What's up, Charlie?

Charlie Well, we're doing interviews for the radio programme for project days. Could I interview you?

Sinan Me? Sure, ok. No problem.

Charlie Alright. Maybe you can tell us your name, your class and the topic of this year's project.

Sinan Yes, my name is Sinan, I'm currently studying in year 8 and the topic ... well, it was all about a social project outside of school.

Charlie Social project outside school ... like what for example?

Sinan Well, good question. Well, we were told we had to find a job, a social job. You know, like in a kindergarten, hospital, something like that. And sort of help out for a couple of days.

Charlie Help out ... So tell us, tell us some more about that.

Sinan Well, ok, we started off in an old people's home. And it wasn't just me. There was Louie was there and Emma and of course myself. We gave them their food, you know, we chatted with them, you know, kept them company, cleaned the rooms, stuff like that. Well, you know, it wasn't easy, it was... sometimes it was pretty hard ... but it was nice to be ... to be needed.

Charlie And now you're back in school.

Sinan Yeah, that's right. And now we're back we're all sort of comparing our experiences and telling everybody about it.

Charlie So, what do you think, was this experience helpful for improving the atmosphere at school or ...

Sinan Yes, I think it was definitively a good experience. You know when you see people in that environment, old people in the home, you know they have no family, they've got no friends ... it makes you realise how lucky we really are and how stupid some of our little fights are, what we have to deal with in school and puts it all into perspective really. So I'd say it definitively helped us in experience.

Charlie Alright, well thanks, Sinan, that was very interesting! Oh, here comes Erin! Erin, could I just stop you for a sec?

Lösungsbeispiel:

1 a social project outside (of) school

2 kindergarten, hospital, old people's home

3 gave food to the old people, talked to them / chatted with them, cleaned rooms, kept the old people company

4 makes students see how lucky they are / how stupid/silly their little fights at school are

2 WORDS Understanding new words

a) tiring: ermüdend; disadvantaged: benachteiligt; relaxed: entspannt

b) rewarding: lohnend/befriedigend/bereichernd; carer: Betreuer(in); (to be) in charge of: verantwortlich sein; plenty of: reichlich; (to) provide: zur Verfügung stellen; (to) benefit: profitieren; confident: selbstsicher

3 LANGUAGE Visitors at Parkside School

1 Harry asked us why we had project days at our school.

2 Mr Dixon asked us if we liked the project days.

3 Amy wanted to know if classes did something different every year.

4 Mrs Smith wanted to know if there were any new ideas for next year.

5 Akim wanted to know how the projects improved the school climate.

6 Ewa asked Mrs Cooper if they could come again next year.

Lerntipp Indirekte Rede (Fragen)

Wenn du Fragen in die indirekte Rede setzt, gelten die gleichen Regeln wie bei Aussagen:

1 Steht das einleitende Verb im *simple past*, so ändern sich die Zeiten in der indirekten Frage *(backshift).*
2 Manchmal musst du die Person (Pronomen) im Fragesatz ändern, je nachdem, wer spricht.
3 Es gilt die gleiche Satzstellung wie in Aussagen (Subjekt – Verb), denn aus der Frage ist nun in der indirekten Rede ein Aussagesatz geworden.
Das Fragewort *(Who…? / What…? /…)* aus der direkten Frage bleibt erhalten.
4 Gibt es in der direkten Frage kein Fragewort, setzt du in der indirekten Frage ein *if* ein.

Beispiele:

direkt	The teacher **asked** Anna: **Is** Ben **your** brother?
indirekt	The teacher **asked** Anna **if** Ben **was her** brother.
direkt	Noah **asked** me: **Where** do **you live**?
indirekt	Noah **asked** me **where I lived**.
direkt	My dad **asked** my friends: Do **you like** soccer?
indirekt	My dad **asked** my friends **if they liked** soccer.

Probiere das gleich einmal an folgenden Sätzen aus:

Jack asked Emily: Do you go shopping a lot?

Mum asked the bus driver: When does the next bus leave?

She asked him: Are you crazy?

Lösung:
Jack asked Emily if she went shopping a lot.
Mum asked the bus driver when the next bus left.
She asked him if he was crazy.

4 WRITING Giving and getting respect in the city

Lösungsbeispiel:

Life in a city is exciting, but sometimes dangerous too. To make life easier and less dangerous for everybody it is important to show respect to each other. In my experience you will get respect if you give respect.

For example, drivers can give respect to slower people like children, old people or people on bikes by driving carefully. And slower people can show respect by paying attention and saying “thank you”. These two words will make the driver give respect to slower people the next time too.

To sum up, there are many situations every day where you can give respect to other people. The more people show respect, the more people will get respect. So why not start today?

Lerntipp *Writing* üben

Gewöhn dir an, vor Schreibaufgaben Ideen zu sammeln. Dies kannst du z.B. mit einer Mindmap tun. Oft hilft dir die Mindmap auch, deine Gedanken und Ideen zu bündeln und zu strukturieren.
Die folgende Struktur eignet sich für Kommentare:
- Einleitung: Hier sagst du, worum es in deinem Text geht. Das kann ein einleitender allgemeiner Satz über das Thema sein, eine Frage und/oder deine Meinung.
- Mittelteil: Hier begründest du deine Meinung mit Argumenten und Beispielen.
- Schluss: Hier ziehst du deine Schlussfolgerungen aus den Argumenten und greifst deine Meinung aus der Einleitung wieder auf.

8 5 SPEAKING Making small talk

Rolecard: João

Your partner starts:
- React to what your partner says.
- Introduce yourself.

Answer your partner's questions, e.g. say:
- where you're from
- why your family came to Germany
- how you like it
- if you've been to Germany before
- what you're interested in

Also ask your partner some questions, e.g.:
- if he/she has already been to Portugal
- what he/she is interested in
- about activities you can do at the school
- about interesting things to see in town
- about how to find your way around school

Be polite! Be positive! Be open!

Lösungsbeispiel:

You	Hi, I'm Paula. Are you the new student?
João	Yes, I'm João. Nice to meet you.
You	Nice to meet you too. Are you in Germany for the first time?
João	Yes, I am. We arrived two weeks ago.
You	You're from Portugal, aren't you? That's what our teacher told us.
João	That's right. I'm from a small town on the coast.
You	So why did your family decide to move to Germany?
João	My dad lost his job in Portugal and couldn't find a new one. So we had to do something.
You	Oh, I'm sorry about that. So has he found a new job here?
João	Yes, he has. He works at the airport.
You	That's great. And what about your mum?
João	My mum is still looking for a job. She's also busy learning German.

You	So how do you like it so far?
João	I really like Cologne and this school seems nice. But I miss my friends.
You	I can imagine. But I'm sure you'll find new friends soon. You know, there are lots of activities that you can do at this school. That's a great way to meet people.
João	That sounds like a great idea. So what activities can you do?
You	You can do lots of sports, like soccer or basketball. And there is a band, for example ... I play in the band.
João	Oh, nice! What instrument do you play?
You	I play the keyboard. And we're always looking for new band members. Do you play an instrument?
João	Yes, I do. I play the guitar.
You	That's great. So why don't you come to band practice after school?
João	Today? Yes, that would be great! Which room do I have to go to?
You	Band practice is in the music room. That's on the second floor, you know?
João	Errr, no, I haven't been there yet. But I can ask.
You	Why don't we go together? We can meet here after school.
João	That would be great – thank you!
You	OK, great. So see you later. Bye!
João	Bye.

6 MEDIATION An adventure activity day at a German school

Lösungsvorschlag:

There was an adventure activity day at our school. It was for 7th graders and it was organized by some experts for adventure activities.

The students had to do twelve different tasks. One task was to climb a high ladder in the trees.

Another task was to dance with a 'blind' partner without talking – you had to show your partner what to do with your body.

The students liked the day a lot. They said that they had learned many new things, but sometimes they had been scared too because some tasks were really difficult.

The teachers and the principal think that the adventure activity day was very successful and they want to organize more in the future.

Klassenarbeit A Lösungen

1 READING Tips for job interviews

a)

1 paragraph F (1 P)

2 paragraphs B, D, G (3 P)

3 paragraph H (1 P)

4 paragraph C, E (2 P)

5 paragraph A (1 P)

b) *Lösungsbeispiel:*

1 Sarah and Alfie talk to Mr Green because many students at their school need tips for their job interviews. / are preparing for their job interviews. / are facing their first job interviews. / feel nervous before a job interview. / are looking for jobs or the chance to get some work experience and need some tips on how to prepare for an interview. / ... (1 P)

2 There are two ways to find out more about the company:

– Read/check/study the company's website. (1 P)

– Speak to / talk to / ask someone who works there. (1 P)

3 When you talk about the website during the interview, say what you found interesting, and why. / show that you know details about it. / don't just say that you found it interesting, but explain why. / you should say what information you found interesting, and why. / ... (1 P)

4 During the interview, it's important to show how your strengths match the skills/strengths asked for in the job description. / are what the company needs. / can help you with a problem at school or somewhere else. / make you stand out. / make you a good candidate for the job. / ... (1 P)

5 To make sure that you are on time for the interview, you should find out how long it takes to get there / check the way to the company / check how (long it takes) to get to the company a few days before the interview and be there 15 minutes early / try to arrive 15 minutes before the interview starts / be punctual / arrive early / ... on the day of the interview. (2 P)

6 At the end of the interview, don't just get up and leave, but ask good questions. / show that you are really interested in / keen on the job. / ask questions about the company, the job, and the team. / ... (1 P)

2 WORDS Words that form groups

words	topic
› earn, budget, overspend, run out of money	› getting on with money
confident, energetic, enthusiastic, reliable (2 P)	qualities (1 P)
stylist, assistant, hotel manager, reporter (2 P)	jobs (1 P)
pay, working hours, shift, breaks (2 P)	information about work (1 P)
reference, cover letter, CV, application form (2 P)	application (1 P)

3 LANGUAGE Questions for the interview

Lösungsvorschläge:

How many hours would I normally work in a day?

Do I need to wear any special clothes for the job?

How many people work here?

When can I start?

What kind of work will I do?

When will you let me know about your decision?

How many children are in each group?

4 WRITING An application letter

Lösungsvorschlag:

Dear Sir/Madam
I am writing about the six-month job in Australia. I saw your advert on your website and I would like to apply as a receptionist.
I am in my final year of school and I am thinking about a career in hotel management. Before I apply to the International School of Hotel Management, I would like to get some more experience on the job.
Last summer I worked in a bed and breakfast for two weeks. My job was to welcome guests, answer calls and take new reservations. I really enjoyed my job, but the bed and breakfast was quite small, so now I would like to work in a bigger hotel.
I'm reliable, friendly and can work well in a team. I speak English, German and Turkish, which will help me communicate with visitors from other countries.
As school will finish by the end of July, I could start working in August. My favourite city would be Perth, but I can also imagine working in other cities on the coast.
I enclose my CV and I'm looking forward to your answer.

Yours faithfully,
Justin Crawford

5 SPEAKING Training for job interviews

9 **a)** *Hörtext und Lösungsvorschlag*:

Manager Hello, and welcome. Please sit down and make yourself comfortable. Did you find our offices right away?

You Yes, I did, thank you. I checked the way last Sunday, so it was quite easy, actually.

Manager Ok, today we want to find out more about you and your skills and work experience. In this job you will need to work with the computer a lot. Tell me, what IT skills do you have?

You I use the computer every day. At school we learned a lot about working with computers and we did all our presentations on a computer. Actually I like it very much and I'm good at using the computer.

Manager Can you tell me about your strengths?

You I'm good at organizing things. At school I was a member of the student council and it was often my job to get things organized. For example I organized the school T-shirt sale last year.

Manager That sounds interesting. What about talking in front of people? Is this something you're comfortable with?

You Well, as a member of the student council I had to talk in front of people quite often. This was never a problem for me.

Manager Can you give me an example?

You As I said, we organized a project to sell school T-shirts. My job was to explain the project at our school assembly and tell students how we wanted to organize the sale. It went really well and the principal was very pleased.

Manager How do you think that someone who knows you well would describe you?

You Well, I'm quite sure that he or she would say that I'm friendly, good at presenting things, and very reliable.

Manager Sometimes you have to fix problems. Which of your strengths do you think will help you to do this?

You I'm a good listener and I think that's necessary to fix any problem.

10 **b)** *Hörtext und Lösungsvorschlag:*

Manager Team work is important in most jobs. When you think about school – what special skills do you have that could help a team become successful?

You Well, I'm good at organizing things and I always have good ideas. I think this helps me when I do team work.

Manager So, when do you think a team is a good team?

You Team work means working together and trying hard to get the best possible result. It means having discussions, listening to each other's opinions and then finding a good way to work together.

Manager Let's talk about other achievements. Can you give us one or two examples, you know, of things that you're really proud of? Think about school or a part-time job you've had.

You Oh yes, I won a prize for the best picture in an art competition. I hadn't expected it, although I've always been quite good at art. That was great. I won a fantastic smartphone.

Manager Why should we choose you for this job?

You Because I'm hard-working, reliable and I think that the skills I described will help me with this job.

Manager Well, thank you very much for your time. We'll contact you again in a few days to let you know our decision.

You Bye and thank you for the interview.

Lerntipp

Nachdem du das *Speaking* beendet hast, kannst du deine Notizen mit den Lösungsvorschlägen vergleichen. Finde heraus, an welchen Stellen du deine Lösung noch verbessern kannst. Ist es ...

- die Satzstellung
- die Zeit
- die Wortwahl
- eine Kurzantwort, die der eigentlichen Antwort vorangestellt ist,
- die Höflichkeit *(please, thank you, ...)*
- ... ?

Präge dir die Verbesserungsvorschläge ein.
Nach einiger Zeit kannst du die Übung wiederholen und dich so verbessern.

Klassenarbeit B Lösungen

1 LISTENING Work experience

a) *Hörtext:*

11

Mr Conkin Alright, hello everybody, can we quieten down a little bit, please. Ok. Now welcome back after a week of work experience. I'm really excited to find out how your weeks went. I want to know how it was for you personally, I want to know good aspects, bad aspects – everything. So who would like to start? Sophie, do you want to go ahead?

Sophie Yeah, ok ... well, I worked at the City Council, I didn't find anything else, so I decided to go there.

Mr Conkin Ok, what was it like for you?

Sophie It was a bit boring ... It was – at the beginning there wasn't very much to do and we were just sitting around. But the people were really nice.

Mr Conkin Ok. What was it exactly that you had to do?

Sophie Well, they were doing this project called "Old people in our town" and the City Council wanted to find out how old people feel and what they need and what they like and don't like ... and ...

Mr Conkin What was your role in the project? What did you have to do?

Sophie Well, I had to read the questionnaires that the old people had to answer. Yeah, that was pretty easy.

Mr Conkin But ... what was difficult?

Sophie Well, the hard bit was that we had to actually ask the people these questions. I had to ... I had to talk to the old people ...

Mr Conkin Ok, you were out on the street talking to strangers. That was a challenge.

Sophie Yeah.

Mr Conkin Ok.

Sophie But you know, I was in a team with six other people and we worked out the questions together and then we went out onto the streets and I was paired up with someone and then we had to do the interviews.

Mr Conkin Ok. And how was that for you? I mean, as you said, you're quite a shy person, so confronting strangers on the street – how was that?

Sophie Really hard in the beginning. I was just really shy and I didn't know what to say and ... – but what was really good was that these people were really friendly and they loved talking to us and they loved answering the questions and ... and I guess with each person I met I got more and more confident and so I ... I actually found that I'm really good at talking to people.

Mr Conkin Do you think this will help you in the future? Do you think it's built up your confidence somewhat?

Sophie Yeah, I think so. And I think when I'm ... – that if I do a job interview or something I might be a bit more prepared for it.

Mr Conkin That's great! So just give me a round up then of some positive and negative aspects.

Sophie Well, I guess the really good thing was that I was treated like an equal, being treated like an adult, so that was really cool. And negative ... well, it was really long days and we only got a short break for lunch.

Mr Conkin Ok, thanks Sophie. It sounds like you had quite a good week! So Liam, why don't you tell us what you got up to this week ...

Lösungsvorschlag:

1 Mr Conkin asks the students to tell the class about their week of work experience / their work experience / good and bad aspects of their work experience. (1 P)

2 Sophie worked at the City Council because she didn't/couldn't find anything else. (1 P)

3 At the beginning it was boring because there wasn't much to do / there was a lot of sitting around. (1 P)

4 The City Council wanted to find out about how old people (0,5 P) feel, what they need, what they like and what they don't like. (0,5 P)

5 At first, interviewing people on the street was hard / difficult / a big challenge (0,5 P) for Sophie because she is shy / she is a shy person / she had to talk to strangers / she didn't know what to say. (0,5 P)

6 But after some interviews, Sophie got more and more confident. (1 P)

7 Sophie found out that she is good at talking to people. (1 P)

8 Sophie didn't like the long working hours / long days (0,5 P) and the short lunch break / short break for lunch. (0,5 P)

b) *Hörtext:*

12

Mr Conkin	So, Liam, why don't you tell us what you got up to this week?
Liam	Ok ... Don't laugh, but I ended up in a flower shop. Not really because I'm specifically interested in flowers, but ... I couldn't find anywhere else for my work experience.
Mr Conkin	Ok. What would have been your favourite place?
Liam	To be honest, I couldn't decide anything!
Mr Conkin	Ok, why was that?
Liam	Well, to be honest, I think I just waited too long to find a place.
Mr Conkin	Ok. Well, you found somewhere in the end. How did you find the flower shop?
Liam	Well, to be honest, my father helped me because the ... it's a friend of the family, you know, the owner, and he just said well, why don't you come to me?
Mr Conkin	Ok, so tell us a bit more.
Liam	Well, it was just me and him. There weren't anybody else ... there wasn't anybody else working there, there was nobody to talk to ... The owner was kind of an old guy, he was about 60. I had to water the plants every morning, you know, change the water, help him with customers, carry heavy stuff, pots and things, watering cans ... Sometimes there was nothing to do at all, so I just read books about plants.
Mr Conkin	Oh well, that sounds like you've made the most of your time!
Liam	Yeah.
Mr Conkin	And what were the working hours like?
Liam	Well, let's see ... I had to be there at half past eight in the morning, then I'd have a break for lunch ... and I usually got to leave about half past five. Something like that.
Mr Conkin	Ok, so a bit of an early start. Just give us a round up then of what you think were the good things and the bad things about your week.

Liam	Well, I think we've already sort of mentioned the bad highlights as it were. Good things ... I know that it's something in the future that I don't want to do. Not working in a shop.
Mr Conkin	That's good.
Liam	Yeah. I really don't want to sell things in the future. But I kind of like plants! It's something I didn't expect, but exotic plants, you know – maybe I could work as a gardener in London or a big park or ... landscaping? Maybe something like that. But an office job – definitively not for me. I'm sort of an outside person.
Mr Conkin	Hey, well, Liam, I'm really pleased that you found something productive out of that week, that's really good! I'm very pleased. Ok ... Tariq, let's continue with you ...

Lösung:

1	Liam worked in a flower shop ...	because he loves flowers.	
		because his favourite shop didn't have work for him.	
		because his father knew the shop owner.	✓
		because of the long lunch break.	
2	During his week in the flower shop, Liam ...	met many different people.	
		did small jobs like watering the plants.	✓
		talked to the owner a lot.	
		had fun with the other employees.	
3	When there wasn't anything special to do for Liam, ...	he went home earlier.	
		he had a longer lunch break.	
		he tried to find out about other jobs.	
		he read a lot about plants.	✓
4	To sum up, Liam says that ...	he experienced mostly bad things.	
		he found out something important for his future.	✓
		he definitely doesn't want to work with plants.	
		maybe an office job would be better for him.	
5	Mr Conkin thinks that ...	Liam used his time well.	✓
		Liam should have worked harder.	
		it's funny that Liam worked in a flower shop.	
		Liam should work in an office.	

2 WORDS Crossword

Across

1 Learning to play an instrument is quite an achievement. (0,5 P)

2 Let's pretend to be happy with the presents and sell them later. (0,5 P)

3 This isn't working. Let's try a different approach. (0,5 P)

6 For some jobs, work experience is absolutely necessary. (0,5 P)

8 If you want to get a good job, it's important to get a good education. (0,5 P)

9 I was afraid she'd be sad, but she's quite cheerful. (0,5 P)

Down

1 Wear clean, ironed clothes at your job interview because your appearance matters. (0,5 P)

4 In my next application I'm going to list my English teacher as a reference. (0,5 P)

5 The opposite of weakness: strength (0,5 P)

7 What you're saying is wrong. It's a lie. (0,5 P)

3 WORDS Explaining words

Lösungsvorschlag:

1 'Pleased' is another word for 'happy'. / 'Pleased' is very similar to 'happy'. / 'Pleased' is the opposite of 'unhappy'. / You say that a person is pleased if he/she is happy with the result of something. / ... (1,5 P)

2 A key is something that you need to open or close a house or a car. / A key is a tool that you use to open a door. / A key is a metal thing that you put into a key hole to open or close a door. / A key is a piece of metal that can open a door. / 'Key' is similar to 'important', for example if you talk about skills that are necessary for a job. / ... (1,5 P)

3 'Confident' is the opposite of 'shy'/'unsure'/'afraid'. / You say that a person is confident if he/she thinks well of himself/herself. / If you are confident, you have the feeling that you can do something well. / To be confident is to like yourself. / ... (1,5 P)

4 A takeaway is a meal that you buy in a shop or restaurant and eat at home or somewhere else. / It's food that is bought in a shop or restaurant, but is not eaten there. / ... (1,5 P)

5 'Appearance' is the way that someone or something looks. / 'Appearance' is the way people look or dress. / 'Appearance' is the way you look to other people. / ... (1,5 P)

6 If you're punctual, you're on time. / 'Punctual' is the opposite of 'late'. / To be punctual is to arrive at the right time. / ... (1,5 P)

4 LANGUAGE A job interview

interview questions	answers
What are your favourite subjects (at school)? / Do you have a favourite subject at school? (1,5 P)	My favourite subjects are science and maths.
When are you going to leave school? (1,5 P)	I'm going to leave school next August.
What/Which language(s) do you speak? / Do you speak any languages? (1,5 P)	I speak French and some German.
Do you (know how to) play an instrument? (1,5 P)	No, I don't. I used to play the guitar a few years ago.
What is your greatest strength? / What do you think is your greatest strength? (1,5 P)	My greatest strength is communication.
Do you have a (part-time) job? / Do you work at the weekend? (1,5 P)	Yes, I do. I work in a shoe shop every second Saturday.
Have you ever worked with children? / Have you worked with children before / in the past? (1,5 P)	Yes, I've worked with children as a baby-sitter and as a volunteer at summer camps.
When can you start (working here)? (1,5 P)	I can start next September.

5 REVISION LANGUAGE An interview for the school magazine (8 P)

Lösungsvorschlag:

1 Do you write every day?

2 When do you normally/usually start working/writing in the morning?

3 Have you ever had a writer's block?

4 Are you working on / writing a new book at the moment / now?

5 What's your new book about?

6 When will your new book come out?

7 How long did it take you to write your last book?

8 How did you get the idea for your last book?

6 WRITING About my work experience

Lösungsvorschlag:

I did my work experience at an old people's home. The morning shift started at 7.30 am, so I had to get up very early every day.

In the mornings I sat with the old people while they ate their breakfast. After that I had to clean the tables and help in the kitchen. Around 10 o'clock it was time for the old people to go outside, so I needed to push those people who were sitting in wheelchairs into the garden.

Lunch was served at 1 pm and after lunch we played board games and told stories. The old people asked me a lot of questions about school and I liked listening to their stories. My shift ended at 4 pm.

At the end of the week I was sad to leave. But my boss said that I could come back anytime to visit!

Lerntipp Aus Fehlern kannst du lernen!

Sieh dir daher deine Lösung noch einmal genau an:
- Unterstreiche jedes Verb. Ist es im *simple past*? Stimmt die Form (regelmäßig oder unregelmäßig)?
- Hast du genügend *time phrases* und *linking words* verwendet? Unterstreiche sie mit einer anderen Farbe und überprüfe so, ob es genügend sind. Überlege, wo du weitere *time phrases* oder *linking words* einfügen könntest, um deinen Text interessanter zu machen.
- An einigen Stellen kann man vielleicht auch einen Relativsatz verwenden, um jemanden oder etwas genauer zu beschreiben.
- Als letzten Punkt solltest du deine Satzstellung überprüfen. In englischen Sätzen gilt die Regel: Subjekt – Verb – Objekt (vgl. *Language file* 11 und 12, SB-Seite 188/189)

7 MEDIATION Talking about jobs at a summer camp (12 P)

Lösungsvorschlag:

	The group leader	The expert
Worin besteht die Aufgabe? (3 Fakten)	• *Man leitet eine Gruppe von Kindern zwischen acht und zwölf Jahren.* • *Man begleitet die Kinder zu Aktivitäten.* • *Man ist der erste Ansprechpartner, wenn es Probleme gibt. / Man hilft den Kindern, ihre Probleme zu lösen.* • *Man plant die Woche im Team mit anderen. / Man entwickelt (zusammen mit anderen) neue Ideen und Pläne für die Woche.*	• *Man ist für eine Aktivität /Sportart verantwortlich.* • *Man coacht/unterstützt/trainiert die Mitarbeiter.* • *Man sorgt dafür, dass die Aktivität beliebt ist.*
Was suchen sie für Leute? (3 Aspekte)	• *Sie suchen begeisterungsfähige Leute / Leute, die gerne Spaß haben.* • *Man sollte aber auch ernst sein können.* • *Man sollte selbstbewusst sein / eine Gruppe führen können.*	• *Man sollte den Sport sehr gut können.* • *Man sollte bereits Erfahrung als Trainer mitbringen.* • *Man sollte hoch motiviert sein.* • *Man sollte gut organisieren können.*

Klassenarbeit A Lösungen

1 READING Mae's blog: How I got into cooking

a) (6 P)

An argument with the principal		Talking to the principal	2
A new lesson at school	6	A big change in year 9	1
The kitchen is too small		Working with time pressure	5
We need a better plan	4	A plan to collect the money	3
Cooking for two days		Ten sponsors can win a prize!	

b) (7 P)

1	Two years ago, some students in Mae's class ...	wanted a bigger school canteen.	
		started a campaign for more vegetables.	
		wanted to cook their own meals at school.	
		complained about the lunch at school.	✓
2	Ms Bloom, the principal, said that ...	she would help them collect the money.	
		Mae and Matteo should focus on school.	
		a new kitchen was too expensive.	✓
		the lunch was good enough for students.	
3	They agreed on a crowdfunding project ...	to find lots of sponsors for the new kitchen.	✓
		because Ahmed wanted to set up a website.	
		because all the other ideas weren't realistic.	
		and decided to give ten pounds each.	
4	As a prize, they offered the sponsors ...	a new kitchen.	
		dinner in a famous restaurant.	
		20,000 £.	
		dinner prepared in the new kitchen.	✓
5	Money started coming in ...	because Matteo's father joined the project.	
		after they posted pictures of their school lunch.	✓
		after a newspaper reported on their project.	
		when Mae opened an online shop.	
6	Matteo, Ahmed and Mae ...	felt frustrated with all they had to do.	
		asked Matteo's father to organize everything.	
		enjoyed preparing the dinner for the sponsors.	✓
		were tired in the evening.	
7	After the dinner ...	Mae, Matteo and Ahmed won a prize.	
		Mae made cooking her hobby.	✓
		Ms Bloom joined a cooking class.	
		they got jobs at *Ristorante Don Camillo*.	

2 WORDS Can you find the words? (6 P)

2 I don't think it's realistic to finish all this homework in just one hour.

3 In other words, I've always been more interested in sports.

4 Their parents didn't allow them to watch TV for a while.

5 In order to be successful, Leah had to think of a new strategy.

6 I don't take long to get ready in the morning because I'm good at multitasking.

7 If you lose your credit card, you should call the bank straight away.

3 WORDS What's the right word? (8 P)

1 Isla spends hours and hours surfing the internet. I think she's a digital drifter.

2 It's not my fault, so please don't blame me!

3 I didn't invite these kids! They gatecrashed my party.

4 After a long day at school you should relax for a while.

5 My friend and I had a terrible argument the other day. But now we're friends again.

6 I like this shirt, but it's too expensive. I'll only buy it if they reduce the price.

7 Adam is so creative. He even made a new invention last year. It's a mini robot.

8 I think that students and teachers should be more respectful to each other.

4 LANGUAGE What would have happened if …?

Conditional sentences type 3, Lösung:

Ist sie im **Nebensatz** ***(if-clause)***? Dann musst du das *past perfect* verwenden.

Ist sie im **Hauptsatz** ***(main clause)***? Dann musst du *would/could(n't)* + *have* + *past participle* verwenden.

a)

1 If the principal had given the students money for the new kitchen, everything would have been easier. (1,5 P)

2 If Mae hadn't posted pictures of the school lunch on their crowdfunding website, they wouldn't have collected enough money. (1,5 P)

3 Nothing would have changed if Mae and Matteo had given up after their talk with the principal. (1,5 P)

b)

1 If Matteo's father hadn't helped them, preparing the sponsors' dinner would have taken even longer. (1,5 P)

2 If the school lunch had been better, Mae wouldn't have discovered her love for cooking. (1,5 P)

3 They could have found even more sponsors if the local newspaper had reported on their project. (1,5 P)

5 MEDIATION A special diary (10 P)

Lösungsvorschlag:

You	I found a very special diary on the internet the other day. I'll show you.
Friend	Why would anybody write about their problems online?
You	Well, this diary is special. It can give an answer to your entry. / gives you an answer. / writes back. / can help you with your problems. / reads your entries and answers them, if you want. / tries to help you with your problems. / ... (1 P)
Friend	Really? That sounds interesting! But who writes those answers? A machine?
You	No, a group of volunteers. / No, there are volunteers. / No, real people working for *Sorgen-Tagebuch*. / No, it's people who want to help. / ... (1 P)
Friend	Wow, that sounds pretty responsible. But what happens if they don't know the answer?
You	They ask professionals/experts for help. (1 P)
Friend	OK. But what about privacy? How do people know their diary entries are safe?
You	They are safe for three reasons: – You get a password. / Your diary is protected by a password. / You have a personal account with a password. / You need a user name and a password to open the diary. / ... (1 P) – The diary is anonymous. / You don't have to give any personal data/information. / ... (1 P) – They don't use external software (that saves information on other servers). (1 P)
Friend	That's good to know. But why do people need an online diary? I mean, can't they just talk to friends or family about their problems?
You	A lot of people are afraid to talk about their problems with their friends or family. / Many people find it difficult to talk about their problems with other people (even on the phone). / Sometimes people feel that they can't talk to their friends or family. / ... (1 P)
Friend	Oh, I see. And I guess once I have my own account, I can open my diary on any computer with an internet connection?
You	Yes, of course, that's another advantage. You just need a user name and password / your login details. (1 P)

Friend	What about designing the diary? I mean, a diary is very personal, so I'd want to make this one look personal, too.
You	They offer / There are many different ways/options/possibilities to design / of designing your personal diary. / This online diary has lots of options to make it more personal. / You can design your diary according to your wishes. /... (1 P)
Friend	Wow, I'm impressed. So how much does it cost?
You	Nothing. / It's (for) free. / It doesn't cost anything – it's free. / ... (1 P)
Friend	Well, I think it's a very good idea. I'll check if there's anything like it in English!

6 SPEAKING Online shopping (16 P)

13

a) *Lösungsbeispiel:* (0,5 P pro Wort/Redewendung, maximal 3 P)

don't have a lot of time to go shopping, don't want to spend my time shopping,

glad that I can buy things on the internet, buy nearly all my stuff online,

best time for online shopping, sometimes they don't fit me, send them back,

have a problem with online shopping, trust a shop, ...

b) *Lösungsbeispiel:* (0,5 P pro Vorteil/Nachteil, maximal 3 P)

online shopping		
	advantages	disadvantages
in the radio discussion	– *you can do it when the shops are closed* – you can do it from home – you can buy lots of different things – it leaves you more free time to do other things – the products are brought to your house	– you can't try on the clothes that you want to buy – you don't know if you can trust the shop
other arguments	– you can read what other people think about the products you want to buy – you can buy things even if you live far away from the shops – ...	– you can't speak with a salesperson – you have to have a credit card – you have to have an internet connection – it's bad for the environment – salespeople lose their jobs – shops have to close and city centres get boring – ...

c) *Lösungsvorschlag:* (10 P)

Hi, I'm Olivia from Germany. I'm 16 years old and I still go to school.

Well, I must say that I quite like online shopping. I know that it can be a problem for real shops because they lose customers and can't pay their rent. But we live in the country and there isn't a good choice of shops here. So when I want to buy something – like books, or sports equipment – I look online. It's easier and faster than going to the city, and you can choose from so many products!

Unfortunately I can't buy things for myself because I don't have my own bank card. So I always have to ask my parents to buy things for me. I don't usually buy clothes on the internet, though, because I like to try them on before I buy them. Yes, I know you can always send them back, but that means packing everything up again, going to the post office and so on. And it's a big waste of fuel to always send things back. I prefer to go to the shopping mall with a friend.

So yes, I do some online shopping and I think it's a great thing if you live in the country. But I try not to do it too much because I know that it has some bad results – for shop owners, for the environment and even for cities. I think it's important that there are still some shops in the cities because it's the shops that make a good city.

Klassenarbeit B Lösungen

1 LISTENING A project about advertisements

a) *Hörtext:*

14 Part 1

Julian Welcome to our presentation about advertisements. Annie, Jared, Amina and I are going to show you some ads that we found in magazines.
OK, here's the first ad. Can you all see it? It shows a very small smoothie bottle. You can tell that it's very small because, right next to it, you can see a lunchbox and the bottle is smaller. In fact, it looks like you could fit the bottle into the lunch box.
There are three kids on the left, we think they're about our age. They're smiling, and they're holding these little smoothie bottles – and they all look quite cool and very happy.
Now look at the slogan. It reads: "A little bit of happiness". That's the simple message of this ad: this small smoothie will bring you happiness. The colours are simple too: the bottle is yellow with a green label saying "Smooth and small". And the lunchbox has the same colours: it's light green with a big yellow smiley on it. Both colours are typical for fruit. Perfect, isn't it?
We like this ad because it's so simple and clear. You see the happy kids holding the smoothie bottles. It looks so easy to be like them – all you have to do is drink this little smoothie.
Well, everybody has to find out if the smoothie really makes them happy. That's up to you, of course. But at least we know that it's healthy!
Now over to Annie.

Part 2

Annie Thanks, Julian.
Well, the next ad is about happiness, too. It's a shopping ad, and it shows four pretty girls, each with a shopping bag from Fashion Passion. Each shopping bag is of a different colour, which might mean that you can buy lots of different things at Fashion Passion. But we're not sure if this is true because we can't see what's in the bags.
The message of the ad is this: shopping at Fashion Passion will make you happy. We think this message is too simple. We also don't like the fact that there are only girls in the ad. This suggests that only girls are interested in fashion and shopping. Of course this isn't true – it's a stereotype. What's more – they all look alike, they don't seem to have individual personalities. **BORING.** No, this ad just doesn't work for us. The message is way too simple and there's nothing about it that will attract young people. We say: thumbs down for this ad. (...) Jared, your turn!

Part 3

Jared Erm ... right. Sorry.
Well, the third ad targets young people from about 10 to about 18 years old. You can tell this from the age of the kids in the ad. The setting is a nice town square with a water fountain. There are three boys and two girls sitting in different places – on a chair, on a skateboard, on a rucksack, on the steps of the fountain – and reading books. They don't seem to be interested in what's going on around them – instead, they're completely focused on reading their books.
OK, so (...) each of them is reading a book and, although we can't really read their titles, we can see that the books are all part of the same series called "Youngbooks". There's a slogan at the top of the ad: "Enjoy Youngbooks". That's all. And that's exactly what we like about it: it's short and simple. Of course part of the message is also that these books are for young people – and that, if you buy a Youngbook, you won't be able to

stop reading. You'll want to read it anytime, anywhere.
Another great thing about this ad is that it shows an unusual scene: lots of young people just sitting around, reading. The situation is a bit strange, and that's what makes it so interesting. And it makes us want to know what's written in these books. Great idea, great ad!
Erm ... now over to Amina.

Part 4

Amina Thanks, Jared.
OK. Our last ad shows a young man running up a hill. He seems to be very fit. You can see this from his perfect body. Well – at least Annie and I think it's a perfect body... Anyway, behind the young man, a bit further down the hill, there are three other people – a girl and two boys. Two of them have stopped running, and they all look very tired. They probably don't have enough energy to continue running. Then, in the bottom left corner of the ad, there's a picture of a drink called Protein Power. Now if you put these things together, the message becomes quite clear: drink Protein Power and you will be unstoppable.
The interesting thing about this ad is that it works without a slogan. You only *see* the *product*. Still, everybody can understand the message. We are sure that this ad will catch the interest of young, sporty people – they might want to try the drink. What about you – would this ad make you buy Protein Power?

The students are talking about ads 2, 3, 5 and 8. (4 P)

Lerntipp Notizen machen

Übe dich im Notieren der Informationen. Dabei ist es am besten, wenn du für dich festlegst, wie du deine Notizen machen willst. Du kannst dir z. B. eigene Abkürzungen ausdenken, die du immer verwendest. Notiere dir die Namen und schreibe alle Zahlen auf, die du hörst. Hast du noch Schwierigkeiten, Zahlen zu verstehen, trainiere dies ganz gezielt.

15

b) *Hörtext:* (part 1 again)

1 You know that the smoothie bottle is very small because it fits into a/the lunch box. / (you can see that) it's smaller than a/the lunch box. / there's a lunch box next to it and the bottle is smaller. / it looks like you could fit the bottle into the lunch box. / the bottle is smaller than the lunch box (next to it). / you can put it in the lunch box. / ... (1 P)

2 The kids in the ad are walking, smiling and drinking the smoothie. / holding (the) smoothie bottles (in their hands). / they have smoothie bottles. / ... (1 P)

3 The main colours of the ad are (light) green and yellow. (1 P)

4 The message of the ad is that if you drink this (small) smoothie, you will be happy. / this (small) smoothie will bring you happiness / will make you happy. / if you want to be happy (like the kids in the ad), all you have to do is drink this (small) smoothie. / the little smoothie can make you happy. / if you drink the smoothie, you will be like the kids: happy and cool. / ... (1 P)

5 Julian and the others like the ad because it's (so) simple and clear. / the colours are perfect. / the message is (so) simple. / it has a simple message. / it's easy to understand. / ... (1 P)

16 **c)** *Hörtext:* (part 2 again)

1 What could the different colours of the shopping bags mean?

(It could/might mean that) you can buy lots of / many different things at Fashion Passion. / (Perhaps it means that) the shop sells many different styles of clothes. / The four girls bought many different things at Fashion Passion. / There are different things in the shopping bags. / ... (1 P)

2 What's the message of the ad?

Shopping at Fashion Passion will make you happy. (1 P)

3 Why does Annie complain that there are only girls in the ad?

It suggests that only girls are interested in fashion and shopping. / It's a stereotype. / The ad makes people believe that only girls are interested in fashion and shopping. / ... (1 P)

4 Why do Annie and the other students think that the ad is boring?

Because the girls all look alike / the same / similar. / Because the girls look like they don't have individual personalities. / Because the girls don't seem to have individual personalities. / Because there's nothing about it that will attract young people. / ... (1 P)

17 **d)** *Hörtext:* (part 3 again) (5 P)

		right	wrong
1	The message of the ad is that reading is strange.		✓
2	The students think that the slogan is too short.		✓
3	The kids in the ad are more interested in their books than in the world around them.	✓	
4	These books will make you addicted to reading.	✓	
5	Jared thinks that the scene shown in the ad is very common.		✓

18 **e)** *Hörtext:* (part 4 again) (4 P)

1	Some of the runners have stopped because …	they don't want to run anymore.	
		they don't have enough energy to continue.	✓
		they haven't practised enough.	
2	The strong runner in the ad …	is doing so well because he has a perfect body.	
		is mean because he doesn't wait for his friends.	
		is unstoppable because he has drunk Protein Power.	✓
3	The message of the ad is that …	drinking Protein Power will make you fit.	✓
		drinking energy drinks is unhealthy.	
		drinking Protein Power will make you good-looking.	
4	Amina and the other students think that the ad …	would work better if it had a slogan.	
		is a bit complicated.	
		might motivate young people to buy the drink.	✓

2 WORDS In English, please!

1 One in three children in the UK / Great Britain have/has never climbed a tree. (1 P)

2 Leave me alone! (1 P)

3 Actually, you're wrong. (1 P)

4 This T-shirt is great, isn't it? (1 P)

5 What are the pros and cons? (1 P)

6 It's a shame / What a shame (that) Lily can't come to the party. (1 P)

3 WORDS Opposites and synonyms

1 (to) pick sth. up ≠ (to) drop sth. (1 P)

2 poor ≠ rich (1 P)

3 until = till (1 P)

4 (to) look for sth. = (to) search for sth. (1 P)

5 (to) say again = (to) repeat (1 P)

6 (to) arrive at a place = (to) reach a place (1 P)

4 LANGUAGE In trouble

1 If she/Julie had written the date into her calendar, she would have remembered it. (2 P)

2 If he/Jacob hadn't talked with his friend Henry, he would have had time to buy it. (2 P)

3 If they / the Connors had taken a taxi, they would have caught the train. (2 P)

4 If I had got *(BE)* / gotten *(AE)* up earlier, I wouldn't have been late for my job interview. (2 P)

5 If Kate had put on a raincoat, she wouldn't have got *(BE)* / gotten *(AE)* a cold. (2 P)

5 REVISION LANGUAGE Talking to a professor

Lösungsvorschlag:

1 According to your research, how many hours a day do teenagers use the internet?
(simple present) (1,5 P)

2 How many boys and girls are addicted to the internet? (simple present) (1,5 P)

3 Have you found out anything new about the risks of using the internet?
(present perfect) (1,5 P)

4 Did you compare the digital habits of different age groups? (simple past) (1,5 P)

5 How can I help if my friend is addicted to the internet? (simple present) (1,5 P)

6 In your opinion, will there still be bookshops in ten years or will everybody use e-books?
(will-future) (1,5 P)

Lerntipp Notizen machen

Bei den Kompetenzen *Speaking* und *Writing* sind Fragen sehr wichtig. Übe daher die richtige Fragebildung immer wieder. Stell dir einfach eine Person vor, die dich interessiert. Überleg dir eine konkrete Situation und stell deiner Person ein paar Interviewfragen. Am besten ist es, wenn du deine Fragen aufschreibst und sie von deiner Lehrerin korrigieren lässt.
Wiederhol diese Übung so oft wie möglich. Beispiele für Übungen:

- Sänger/Sängerin – über das letzte Konzert
- Lehrer/Lehrerin – über seinen/ihren Beruf
- Lieblingssportler/Lieblingssportlerin – über das tägliche Training

6 WRITING Shopping on Sundays around the world (15 P)

Lösungsvorschlag:

Dear E-Teenworld

I'm Lasse (15) and I live in a small town near Hamburg. Usually shops are closed here on Sundays. But some people say that the shops should stay open all weekend.

On the one hand, many people don't have time to go shopping on weekdays and therefore they should have the chance to go on Sundays. To be honest, I've sometimes wished that I could go shopping on Sundays too.
On the other hand we should think about the people who work in the shops. They should have a free day too. And if everybody has the same day off, they can spend time with their friends and family.
To sum up, I think it's best for everybody if the shops stay closed on Sundays.

12

b) Listen to the second part and tick (✓) the correct ending. ____/5

1	Liam worked in a flower shop ...	because he loves flowers.	
		because his favourite shop didn't have work for him.	
		because his father knew the shop owner.	
		because of the long lunch break.	
2	During his week in the flower shop, Liam ...	met many different people.	
		did small jobs like watering the plants.	
		talked to the owner a lot.	
		had fun with the other employees.	
3	When there wasn't anything special to do for Liam, ...	he went home earlier.	
		he had a longer lunch break.	
		he tried to find out about other jobs.	
		he read a lot about plants.	
4	To sum up, Liam says that ...	he experienced mostly bad things.	
		he found out something important for his future.	
		he definitely doesn't want to work with plants.	
		maybe an office job would be better for him.	
5	Mr Conkin thinks that ...	Liam used his time well.	
		Liam should have worked harder.	
		it's funny that Liam worked in a flower shop.	
		Liam should work in an office.	

2 WORDS Crossword

____/5

Find the words and write them into the crossword.

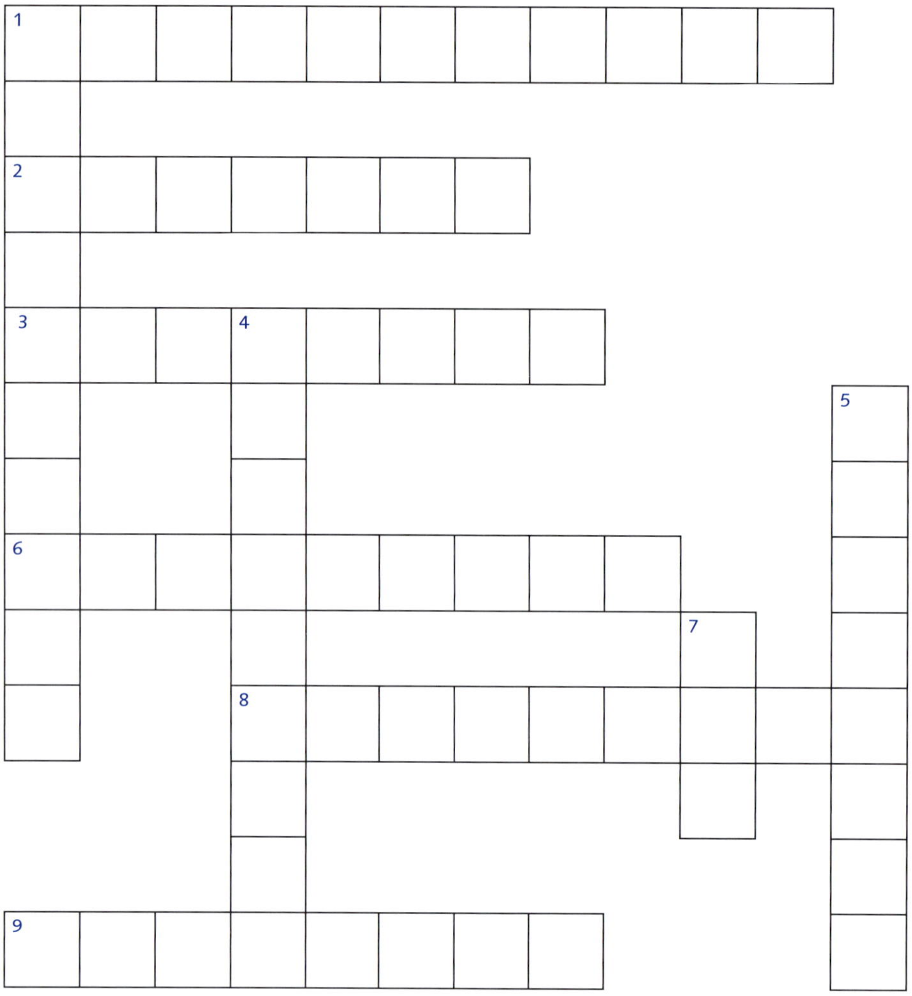

Across

1 Learning to play an instrument is quite an ...
2 Let's ... to be happy with the presents and sell them later.
3 This isn't working. Let's try a different ...
6 For some jobs, work experience is absolutely ...
8 If you want to get a good job, it's important to get a good ...
9 I was afraid she'd be sad, but she's quite ...

Down

1 Wear clean, ironed clothes at your job interview because your ... matters.
4 In my next application I'm going to list my English teacher as a ...
5 The opposite of weakness: ...
7 What you're saying is wrong. It's a ...

3 WORDS Explaining words

_____/9

Explain the following words in one or two sentences.

☞ Es gibt verschiedene Möglichkeiten, ein Wort zu erklären:

1 mit gegensätzlichen Wörtern, z. B. *It's the opposite of …, It means you're not …, It means you don't …*

2 mit gleichen oder ähnlichen Wörtern, z. B. *It's the same as …, … is similar to …*

3 mit Vergleichen, z. B. *It works like …*

4 mit Relativsätzen:
a) bei Personen: *… is a person who …, It's somebody who …*
b) bei Gegenständen: *… is something that …, It's a … that …*
c) bei Orten: *It's a place that … / where …*

5 mit einem Beispielsatz: *If you …, you ….*

1 pleased: ______________________________

2 key: ______________________________

____

3 confident: ______________________________

4 takeaway: ______________________________

____

5 appearance: ______________________________

6 punctual: ______________________________

4 LANGUAGE A job interview

_____/12

More help p. 66

Megan has just had her first job interview. She wants to learn from the interview, so she writes down everything she remembers. Look at Megan's answers (p. 40) and fill in the questions that you think the interviewer asked her.

☞ Sieh dir immer die Antworten genau an und achte dabei besonders auf das Verb und die Zeit, in der es steht. Du musst deine Frage in dieser Zeit stellen.

interview questions	answers
	My favourite subjects are science and maths.
	I'm going to leave school next August.
	I speak French and some German.
	No, I don't. I used to play the guitar a few years ago.
	My greatest strength is communication.
	Yes, I do. I work in a shoe shop every second Saturday.
	Yes, I've worked with children as a babysitter and as a volunteer at summer camps.
	I can start next September.

5 REVISION LANGUAGE An interview for the school magazine ____/8

Your favourite British author is going to visit your school. You want to interview her for the school magazine. Look at your notes and write eight questions in English.

Unbedingt fragen:

- *ob sie jeden Tag schreibt*
- *wann sie normalerweise morgens zu arbeiten beginnt*
- *ob sie jemals eine Schreibblockade (writer's block) hatte*
- *ob sie gerade an einem neuen Buch schreibt*
- *wovon ihr neues Buch handelt*
- *wann ihr neues Buch herauskommen (come out) wird*
- *wie lange sie dafür gebraucht hat, ihr letztes Buch zu schreiben*
- *wie sie die Idee zu ihrem letzten Buch bekam*

1 ____?

2 ____?

3 ____?

4 ____?

5 ____?

6 ____?

7 ____?

8 ____?

6 WRITING About my work experience

____/15

You've just done a week of work experience. Write a report about it (120–140 words).

You can write about:
- where you did your work experience
- the working hours
- your first day
- the team
- what you had to do
- what you liked or didn't like

☞ Sammle deine Ideen und ordne sie, bevor du mit dem Schreiben beginnst.

Denk an *time phrases (first, after that, at 7 o'clock, ...)* und *linking words (and, but, because, ...)*. Deinen Text schreibst du im *simple past*.

7 MEDIATION Talking about jobs at a summer camp ___/12

You're planning a trip to Australia where you want to work at a summer camp. Your grandma wants to know everything about the available jobs, so you show her the organization's website. Tell her the most important facts about each job offer in German. You can use the table on p. 43.

JOBS in AUSTRALIA

Search

Jobs | Volunteering | Community | Service | Contact

DOWN UNDER Summer camps

➡ The group leader

As a group leader you're in charge of a group of kids during their activities in the camp. The kids are between 8 and 12 years old. You will lead your group to the different activities offered in our camp. You should be able to make people laugh and feel good. But you're also the person that kids can talk to whenever there is a problem. So be prepared to fix any kind of problem.

Your day will be full of fun – every day will be different and bring new challenges for you. You need to be flexible and find out about the kids' needs.

You will be working in a team to work out new ideas and plans for every week.

We're looking for enthusiastic people who want to have fun, but can also be strict if necessary. You need to be confident – you're the leader of the group and the kids know this!

If you think that you're the right person for the job, please go ahead and fill in the application form!

➡ The expert

As an expert you will be responsible for a certain activity or sport at the camp. You're the head of the activity or sport and your team includes quite a lot of people. You're responsible for finding ways to make your activity interesting and attractive for the kids. You train the staff and support them to make the most of their training.

We're looking for people who are highly motivated and able to do their activity or sport at a professional level. You should have experience coaching or teaching people as well as organizing activities and planning other fun things. Your job at our camp includes a lot of responsibility, so you will be paid more than most other people working in the camp.

If your skills match this description, please fill in the application form!

	The group leader	The expert
Worin besteht die Aufgabe? (3 Fakten)	• ___ ___ ___ ___ • ___ ___ ___ ___ • ___ ___ ___ ___	• ___ ___ ___ ___ • ___ ___ ___ ___ • ___ ___ ___ ___
Was suchen sie für Leute? (3 Aspekte)	• ___ ___ ___ ___ • ___ ___ ___ ___ • ___ ___ ___ ___	• ___ ___ ___ ___ • ___ ___ ___ ___ • ___ ___ ___ ___

Klassenarbeit A

Gesamtpunktzahl ______/62 Note ______

1 READING Mae's blog: How I got into cooking

Mae, 16, has a food blog that is popular with teens. Read her latest entry.

Welcome to Mae's blog   Tips | Recipes | Archive | Search

1. People often ask me why and how I got into cooking. Well, it all started two years ago, in year 9. One day, during a class meeting, a discussion came up about the quality of the lunch served in our school canteen. And sure enough, the food isn't fresh and often it's even cold. Eating good and healthy food had always been important to me, so I agreed that this was an issue. Then my friend Matteo had an idea. He said that if the school had a real kitchen, we could have a fresh and warm lunch every day. The school canteen is huge and there would be enough space for a kitchen.

______

2. The next day Matteo and I went to see the principal, Ms Bloom. We told her that many students were unhappy with their school lunch and we explained Matteo's idea to build a kitchen in the school canteen. Ms Bloom said that she liked the idea a lot, but that it wasn't realistic because the school just didn't have enough money for a new kitchen. I felt sad and disappointed. If only there was a way for us students to collect the money!

______

3. Before our next class meeting, I did some research. I found out that a kitchen would cost the school 20,000 £. So we would need about 2,000 people to give 10 £ each. How could we possibly get so much money? That was when the idea of starting a crowdfunding project was born. In other words, we would need a website where people could send us money online. Of course people would also need a reason to give us money. Ahmed suggested that we put the names of all our sponsors in a box. Then we could pick the names of five winners and cook a dinner for them in our new kitchen. Brilliant! We set up our website that same day.

______

4. For a while we didn't have many sponsors on our website. So we tried a different strategy: we posted pictures of our school lunch online to show why we really needed a kitchen – the food didn't look very good! We also posted our crowdfunding website on all our Facebook pages. This way we got many sponsors within a short period of time and after three months we had collected 20,000 £. What a good feeling to be successful at last!

______

5. A few weeks after we had our new kitchen, it was time to prepare our sponsors' dinner. With the help of Matteo's father, who is a professional cook at *Ristorante Don Camillo*, Matteo, Ahmed and I created a five-course menu. We made a shopping list, went to the market to buy fresh ingredients and spent the whole day cooking. It was a lot of work and we had to really multitask to finish everything on time. But it was so much fun, and the dinner was a great success with our sponsors!

______

6. After the dinner, Ms Bloom said that we could use the kitchen for cooking classes. Matteo's father offered to teach a class called "Fun with food" – I signed up straight away. Now, every Wednesday, Matteo's father comes to our school and teaches us about food and cooking. And the best recipes and pictures end up on my food blog for you to enjoy! And that's the story of how I discovered my love for cooking. Every week, I look forward to my cooking class and of course, every day, I look forward to a warm and healthy school lunch.

a) Read the text and find the best heading for each paragraph. Write the numbers of the paragraphs in the boxes. There are more headings than you need. ____/6

An argument with the principal		Talking to the principal	
A new lesson at school		A big change in year 9	
The kitchen is too small		Working with time pressure	
We need a better plan		A plan to collect the money	
Cooking for two days		Ten sponsors can win a prize!	

b) Tick (✓) the best sentence ending. ____/7

1	Two years ago, some students in Mae's class ...	wanted a bigger school canteen.	
		started a campaign for more vegetables.	
		wanted to cook their own meals at school.	
		complained about the lunch at school.	
2	Ms Bloom, the principal, said that ...	she would help them collect the money.	
		Mae and Matteo should focus on school.	
		a new kitchen was too expensive.	
		the lunch was good enough for students.	
3	They agreed on a crowdfunding project ...	to find lots of sponsors for the new kitchen.	
		because Ahmed wanted to set up a website.	
		because all the other ideas weren't realistic.	
		and decided to give ten pounds each.	
4	As a prize, they offered the sponsors ...	a new kitchen.	
		dinner in a famous restaurant.	
		20,000 £.	
		dinner prepared in the new kitchen.	
5	Money started coming in ...	because Matteo's father joined the project.	
		after they posted pictures of their school lunch.	
		after a newspaper reported on their project.	
		when Mae opened an online shop.	
6	Matteo, Ahmed and Mae ...	felt frustrated with all they had to do.	
		asked Matteo's father to organize everything.	
		enjoyed preparing the dinner for the sponsors.	
		were tired in the evening.	
7	After the dinner ...	Mae, Matteo and Ahmed won a prize.	
		Mae made cooking her hobby.	
		Ms Bloom joined a cooking class.	
		they got jobs at *Ristorante Don Camillo*.	

2 WORDS Can you find the words?

____/6

Read the sentences below. What do the underlined words and phrases mean? Find words or phrases in Mae's blog that mean more or less the same and complete the sentences.

☞ Achte bei diesem Aufgabentyp darauf, die gefundenen Wörter nicht einfach aus dem Text zu übernehmen. Manchmal musst du sie noch in die dem Satz entsprechende grammatische Form bringen, z.B. in die richtige Zeit.

		paragraph
1	› If this question is discussed at the next meeting, please let me know. = If this question *comes up* at the next meeting, please let me know.	1
2	I don't think it's possible to finish all this homework in just one hour. = I don't think it's ____________ to finish all this homework in just one hour.	2
3	Let me say it this way, I've always been more interested in sports. = ____________, I've always been more interested in sports.	3
4	Their parents didn't allow them to watch TV for some time. = Their parents didn't allow them to watch TV ____________.	4
5	In order to be successful, Leah had to think of a new plan. = In order to be successful, Leah had to think of a new ____________.	4
6	I don't take long to get ready in the morning because I'm good at doing many things at the same time. = I don't take long to get ready in the morning because I'm good at ____________.	5
7	If you lose your credit card, you should call the bank very quickly. = If you lose your credit card, you should call the bank ____________.	6

3 WORDS What's the right word?

____/8

Read the sentences and complete them with words from the box. There are more words than you need.

argument • savvy • relax • irritate • respectful • express • fault • shame • digital drifter • addicted • reduce • invention • gatecrashed • advertiser

1 Isla spends hours and hours surfing the internet. I think she's a ____________.

2 It's not my ____________, so please don't blame me!

3 I didn't invite these kids! They ____________ my party.

4 After a long day at school you should ____________ for a while.

5 My friend and I had a terrible ________________ the other day. But now we're friends again.

6 I like this shirt, but it's too expensive. I'll only buy it if they ________________ the price.

7 Adam is so creative. He even made a new ________________ last year. It's a mini robot.

8 I think that students and teachers should be more ________________ to each other.

4 LANGUAGE What would have happened if …?

More help p. 67

Conditional sentences type 3

Überlege zuerst, in welchem Teil des Satzes die Lücke ist, die du vervollständigen musst.

Ist sie im **Nebensatz** ***(if-clause)***? Dann musst du das *p _ _ _ p _ _ _ _ _ _* verwenden.

Ist sie im **Hauptsatz** ***(main clause)***? Dann musst du *would/could(n't)* + _ _ _ _ + *past participle* verwenden.

Sowohl der Hauptsatz als auch der *if*-Satz können am Anfang oder am Ende des Satzgefüges stehen.

a) Complete the sentences (main clause) with the verb in brackets. ____/4,5

1 If the principal had given the students money for the new kitchen, everything

________________ easier. (be)

2 If Mae hadn't posted pictures of the school lunch on their crowdfunding website, they

________________ enough money. (not collect)

3 Nothing ________________ if Mae and Matteo had given up after their

talk with the principal. (change)

b) Complete the sentences (if-clause) with the verb in brackets. ____/4,5

1 If Matteo's father ________________ them, preparing the sponsors' dinner would

have taken even longer. (not help)

2 If the school lunch ________________ better, Mae wouldn't have discovered her

love for cooking. (be)

3 They could have found even more sponsors if the local newspaper ________________

on their project. (report)

5 MEDIATION A special diary ____/10

You've found a very special online diary on the internet – the *Sorgen-Tagebuch*. Read it and tell your English friend about it.

Sorgen-Tagebuch So funktioniert's | Über uns | Soforthilfe | Anmelden | Suchen

Dein Sorgen-Tagebuch

Teile deine Sorgen & Ängste mit deinem Online-Tagebuch – und es antwortet dir!

Schreibe Tagebuch ...

Gestalte dein ganz persönliches Tagebuch und vertraue ihm deine Sorgen, Ängste, Wünsche und Probleme an!

... erhalte Antworten

Dein Tagebuch liest deine Einträge, und wenn du möchtest, erhältst du eine ganz persönliche Antwort! Dein Tagebuch hört dir zu und versucht zu helfen.

100 % anonym & kostenlos

Das Tagebuch ist kostenlos und völlig anonym. Du musst keine persönlichen Daten angeben!

Wie hilft das Sorgen-Tagebuch?

Die zentrale Idee des Sorgen-Tagebuchs ist es, dass es vielen Leuten hilft, über ihre Probleme zu sprechen – sie sich jedoch nicht trauen, dies vor Freunden oder Verwandten zu tun. Auch der Griff zum Telefon ist meist mit Überwindung verbunden. Was liegt da näher, als seine Sorgen dem guten alten Tagebuch anzuvertrauen? Wir versprechen 100 % Anonymität und versuchen in Form des interaktiven Online-Tagebuchs, ein offenes Ohr für die Probleme unserer Nutzer zu haben und dabei – anders als im herkömmlichen Tagebuch – den Nutzern zu zeigen, dass sich unser Tagebuch für ihre Probleme interessiert.

Wer ist das Sorgen-Tagebuch?

Der Sorgen-Tagebuch e. V. wird dabei von freiwilligen Helfern betreut, die in viel Arbeit einzeln auf die Einträge der Nutzer eingehen. Gemeinsam versuchen wir, die Probleme anzugehen und eine Hilfestellung zu geben. Unsere Helfer beschäftigen sich mit jedem Problem und versuchen nach Möglichkeit zu helfen. Bei Bedarf stehen uns professionelle Berater zur Seite.

Wie funktioniert das Sorgen-Tagebuch?

Dein Tagebuch anlegen

Du kannst auf unserer Seite kostenlos dein eigenes Online-Tagebuch anlegen. Mit deinen Zugangsdaten (Benutzername + Passwort) als Schlüssel kannst du dein Tagebuch jederzeit von überall aufschlagen.

Dein Tagebuch gestalten

Wir bieten verschiedenste Möglichkeiten, wie du dein Tagebuch und deine Einträge nach deinen Wünschen anpassen kannst. Dein Tagebuch ist völlig individuell – du hast zahlreiche Gestaltungsmöglichkeiten!

Antworten erhalten

Auf Wunsch werden unsere Mitarbeiter und ehrenamtlichen Helfer deine Texte lesen und dir Antworten hinterlassen. Wir möchten dich mit deinen Sorgen und Problemen nicht alleine lassen.

Sicherheit & Datenschutz

Datenschutz wird bei uns großgeschrieben! Wir verwenden keine externe Software, die deine Daten oder Informationen über deinen Besuch auf fremden Servern speichert. Deine Texte sind bei uns sicher.

These words might be useful:
anonym – *anonymous*
Zugangsdaten – *login details*
Benutzername – *user name*
Passwort – *password*
Daten – *data*
Server – *server*
Software – *software*
speichern – *save*
extern – *external*

You I found a very special diary on the internet the other day. I'll show you.
Friend Why would anybody write about their problems online?
You Well, this diary is special. It ______________________________
____
______________________________.
Friend Really? That sounds interesting! But who writes those answers? A machine?
You ______________________________.
Friend Wow, that sounds pretty responsible. But what happens if they don't know the answer?
You ______________________________.
Friend OK. But what about privacy? How do people know their diary entries are safe?
You They are safe for three reasons:
– ______________________________.
– ______________________________.
– ______________________________.
Friend That's good to know. But why do people need an online diary? I mean, can't they just talk to friends or family about their problems?
You ______________________________
______________________________.
Friend Oh, I see. And I guess once I have my own account, I can open my diary on any computer with an internet connection?
You Yes, of course, that's another advantage. You just need ______________________________
______________________________.
Friend What about designing the diary? I mean, a diary is very personal, so I'd want to make this one look personal too.
You ______________________________
______________________________.
Friend Wow, I'm impressed. So how much does it cost?
You ______________________________.
Friend Well, I think it's a very good idea. I'll check if there's anything like it in English!

6 SPEAKING Online shopping

There's a discussion on the radio about the advantages and disadvantages of online shopping. People call in to talk about their shopping habits: what they buy or don't buy on the internet, when they buy things online and what they think about online shopping.

13

a) Listen to the first caller. Write down some useful words and phrases. ____/3

buy things on the internet, ______________________

____

____

b) Listen again and note some arguments. Can you think of more arguments for or against online shopping? You can look up words in a dictionary. ____/3

online shopping		
	advantages	**disadvantages**
in the radio discussion	*– you can do it when the shops are closed*	
other arguments		

c) Now you ____/10

Call the radio and talk to the radio presenter for about two minutes:

Tell us something about yourself.

So what are your online shopping habits?

Have you ever bought anything online?

What did you buy and why?

...

Do you think online shopping is a good or a bad thing? Why?

Have you ever had a problem with online shopping?

Does your family buy things online? Why (not)?

Klassenarbeit B

Gesamtpunktzahl ______/68 Note ______

1 LISTENING A project about advertisements

Four students at Parkside School have done a project on ads that target young people. Today they are presenting their results to the rest of the class.

14 **a)** Look at the ads. Then listen to the four presentations and tick (✓) the four ads that the students are talking about.

Mache dir während des Hörens Notizen.

____/4

1

2

3

4

5

6

7

8

b) Listen to Julian's presentation again and finish the sentences with the missing information. ____/5

15

1 You know that the smoothie bottle is very small because ______________________________

______________________________.

2 The kids in the ad are walking, smiling and ______________________________.

3 The main colours of the ad are ______________________________.

4 The message of the ad is that ______________________________

______________________________.

5 Julian and the others like the ad because ______________________________.

c) Listen to Annie's presentation again and answer the questions. ____/4

16

1 What could the different colours of the shopping bags mean?

____

2 What's the message of the ad?

____

3 Why does Annie complain that there are only girls in the ad?

____

4 Why do Annie and the other students think that the ad is boring?

____

d) Listen to Jared's presentation again. Then tick (✓) right or wrong. ____/5

17

		right	wrong
1	The message of the ad is that reading is strange.		
2	The students think that the slogan is too short.		
3	The kids in the ad are more interested in their books than in the world around them.		
4	These books will make you addicted to reading.		
5	Jared thinks that the scene shown in the ad is very common.		

18 **e)** Listen to Amina's presentation again and finish the sentences with the correct endings. ____/4

1	Some of the runners have stopped because …	they don't want to run anymore.	
		they don't have enough energy to continue.	
		they haven't practised enough.	
2	The strong runner in the ad …	is doing so well because he has a perfect body.	
		is mean because he doesn't wait for his friends.	
		is unstoppable because he has drunk Protein Power.	
3	The message of the ad is that …	drinking Protein Power will make you fit.	
		drinking energy drinks is unhealthy.	
		drinking Protein Power will make you good-looking.	
4	Amina and the other students think that the ad …	would work better if it had a slogan.	
		is a bit complicated.	
		might motivate young people to buy the drink.	

2 WORDS In English, please! ____/6

Denk daran, nicht nur die Wörter in der linken Spalte des *Vocabulary* zu lernen, sondern immer auch die Wendungen in der rechten Spalte und in den blauen Kästen.

Was sagst du auf Englisch, wenn du …

1 *sagen willst, dass eins von drei Kindern in Großbritannien noch nie auf einen Baum geklettert ist?*

____

2 *zu deiner Freundin sagen willst, dass sie dich in Ruhe lassen soll?*

____

3 *jemanden höflich darauf hinweisen willst, dass er/sie eigentlich Unrecht hat?*

____

4 *sagen willst: „Dieses T-Shirt ist toll, oder?“?*

____

5 *nach dem Für und Wider fragen willst?*

____

6 *sagen willst, dass es schade ist, dass Lily nicht zur Party kommen kann?*

____

3 WORDS Opposites and synonyms

_____/6

Find the opposite (≠) or the synonym (=) of the following words:

1 (to) pick sth. up ≠ ____________________

2 poor ≠ ____________________

3 until = ____________________

4 (to) look for sth. = ____________________

5 (to) say again = ____________________

6 (to) arrive at a place = ____________________

☞ Achte bei Aufgaben dieses Typs darauf, dass du wirklich die genaue Entsprechung für das vorgegebene Wort aufschreibst, einschließlich eventueller Präpositionen oder Objekte. Wenn z.B. ein Synonym für *(to) greet sb.* gesucht wird, lautet die Entsprechung *(to) say hello* ***to sb.***

4 LANGUAGE In trouble

_____/10

What could they have done to get things right? Make conditional sentences (type 3).

More help p. 68

1 Julie forgot to call her grandma on her birthday.

If – write – the date into her calendar – remember it.

____

2 Jacob didn't have time to buy bread for the family.

If – not talk – with his friend Henry – have time to buy it.

____

3 The Connors missed their train.

If – take a taxi – catch the train.

____

4 I was late for my job interview.

If – get up earlier – not be late for my job interview.

____

5 Kate got a terrible cold.

If – put on a raincoat – not get a cold.

____

5 REVISION LANGUAGE Talking to a professor

____/9

You have the chance to meet Susan Pey, a professor at a British university, who does research on young people and their digital habits. Ask Ms Pey six questions about her work and what she has found out. Use three different tenses.

You could ask her about:

- chances and risks of using digital media
- her research and results
- statistical data (age? boys/girls? number of interviews? etc.)
- her opinion or advice

1 ____?

2 ____?

3 ____?

4 ____?

5 ____?

6 ____?

6 WRITING Shopping on Sundays around the world

____/15

The English e-zine E-TEENWORLD has started a discussion about shopping on Sundays in different countries. You're interested in the topic, so you decide to write an email to E-TEENWORD. Tell them your opinion – should shops stay open on Sundays? Why (not)? What's the situation in your town or city? Write about 120–140 words.

☞ Mach eine Stoffsammlung zum Thema und sammle Argumente für und gegen die Ladenöffnung am Sonntag, bevor du mit dem Schreiben beginnst. Dabei kann dir eine Mindmap helfen. Denk daran, deinen Text sinnvoll zu gliedern. Du brauchst:
- eine Einleitung: Worum geht es in deinem Text? (hier: Wer bist du, wo kommst du her und wie ist die Regelung dort?)
- einen Mittelteil: Was sind die Argumente (pro und contra)?
- eine Schlussfolgerung: Zu welchem Ergebnis kommst du?

Dear E-Teenworld

I'm ____________________ and I live in ____

____

____

____

____

____

____

____

____

____

____

____

____

More help **5** **MEDIATION Dangers at the beach**

___/8

▸ p. 9/10

You are staying with a family in Australia for a few months. Today you are at the beach with your Australian family and you meet a German couple (Herr and Frau Koch). They have lots of questions that your host sister, Chloe, tries to answer. You help with the English and the German.

Perspektivwechsel

Bei *Mediation*-Aufgaben musst du beachten, für wen du sprichst. Die folgende Situation soll dir dies verdeutlichen:

Du bist mit Fabian, einem deutschen Freund, in Australien am Strand. Fabian möchte ein Surfboard leihen und bittet dich, ihm zu helfen.

Fabian: Sag der Frau vom Verleih bitte, dass ich das Surfboard gerne für den ganzen Tag nehmen möchte.

In diesem Fall musst du auf Englisch vermitteln und sagen:

He*'d like to take the surfboard for the whole day.* – und nicht:
I*'d like to take ...*, denn du möchtest das Surfboard ja nicht leihen.

Frau Koch: *Wir sind erst gestern angekommen und haben ein paar Fragen. Gibt es irgendwelche Sicherheitsvorschriften, die wir am Strand beachten müssen?*

Du: ______________________________

____

______________________________ (1,5 P)

Chloe: Well, the sea at some of the most famous beaches can be very dangerous. But there are lifeguards at these beaches, so you should always stay near them. Also you should watch the flags: always swim in the area between the red and the yellow flags. That's the safest area.

Du: ______________________________

____

____

______________________________ (2,5 P)

Frau Koch: *Und wie ist es mit den Haien? Wir haben schon etwas Angst vor Haiangriffen.*

Du: ______________________________ (0,5 P)

Chloe: Again you should only swim at beaches with lifeguards. Never swim in the dark, or in the early morning. Don't swim too far out into the sea and don't swim near rivers.

Du	____
	____
	____ (1,5 P)
Herr Koch	*Was müssen wir noch beachten?*
Du	____ (0,5 P)
Chloe	The sun is very strong in Australia. So always protect your skin with strong suncream, wear a hat and long shirts. You shouldn't stay out in the sun the whole day.
Du	____
	____
	____ (1,5 P)
Frau Koch	*Puh, da muss man schon auf einiges aufpassen. Aber ich danke euch beiden ganz herzlich für eure Hilfe.*
Du	*Bitte, gern geschehen.* Thanks for your help, Chloe.

These words and phrases can help you:

safety rule • follow the rules • shark attacks • keep in mind • whole day • lifeguards – *Rettungsschwimmer* • area – *Gebiet* • also – *außerdem*

More help 6 WRITING Jill's day in the snow

____/10

▸ p. 15

Look at the pictures and imagine you are Jill. Write about the snow in Canberra last week. The phrases can help you. Write about 120 words.

1

Tuesday evening:
announce – snow – excited

2

Wednesday morning:
next morning – look – no snow – disappointed

3

At school: finally – start to snow – watch

4

5

After school:
play – snowball fight – snowman – take/send photos

6

Wednesday evening:
in the evening – cold – warm up – barbecue

7

Thursday morning:
next morning – snow – gone – photos – remember

Drei Tipps für einen gelungenen Text:

1 Achte auf die richtigen Zeiten.
2 Beschreibe Jills Gefühle.
3 Verwende *time phrases* und *linking words*.

You can start like this:

Last Tuesday the weather forecast announced

More help **3** **LANGUAGE A class discussion about bullying** ____/4

▸ p. 18/19

a) Here's what some kids said about bullying. Put their sentences into indirect speech. Remember to change the underlined words.

Indirekte Rede (Aussagesätze und Fragen)

Wenn du einen Aussage- oder Fragesatz aus der direkten Rede in die indirekte Rede setzen willst, musst du zwei Dinge bedenken:

1. In welcher Zeit steht das einleitende Verb? *(say, complain, ask, ...)*
   Steht es im *simple past*, so ändern sich die Zeiten in der indirekten Rede *(backshift)*.
2. Muss man Personen (Pronomen) ändern?
   Wenn in der direkten Rede ein Pronomen steht, ändert es sich manchmal in der indirekten Rede.

Katie

① Some of my classmates call me names.

② Jack and Igor make fun of me.

Ethan

1 *Katie said that* ______________________________

2 *Ethan complained that* ______________________________

Molly

③ Jessica sometimes kicks me.

④ I get mean text messages again and again.

Omar

3 *Molly said* ______________________________

4 *Omar* ______________________________

More help 3 LANGUAGE Visitors at Parkside School

____/9

▸ p. 25

There are visitors at Parkside School. They are teachers and students from another school and want to learn more about the project days. Write their questions. Pay attention to the underlined words.

Indirekte Rede (Fragen)

Wiederhole kurz die Eckpunkte der indirekten Fragen, bevor du mit der Aufgabe beginnst:

- Wie verändert sich die Zeit?
- Was muss man oft auch noch verändern?
- Wie verändert sich die Satzstellung?
- Wann muss man ein zusätzliches Wort einfügen?

Harry

1 Why do you have project days at your school?

Harry asked us ____________________

____

____

Mr Dixon

2 Do you like the project days?

Mr Dixon asked us ____________________

____

____

Amy

3 Do classes do something different every year?

Amy wanted to know ____________________

____

____

Mrs Smith

4 Are there any new ideas for next year?

Mrs Smith wanted to know ____________________

____

____

Akim

5 How do the projects improve the school climate?

Akim wanted to know ____________________

____

____

Ewa

6 Mrs Cooper, can we come again next year?

Ewa asked Mrs Cooper ____________________

____

____

More help **4** **WRITING Giving and getting respect in the city**

Look at the poster and think of different situations where respect in the city is important. Then follow the five steps on p. 63 and write a comment about what respect in the city means to you. Write about 100–120 words.

____/12

▶ p. 26

Step 1: Before you start writing, collect ideas in a **mind map** and choose one or two situations.

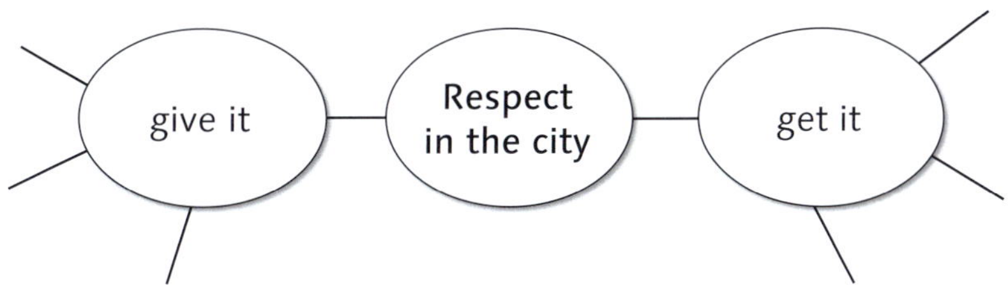

Step 2: beginning: Think of one or two good sentences to introduce your topic. This can be:
- a general statement, e.g. about life in a city
- a question that you want to answer in your text
- your opinion

____

____

Step 3: middle: Describe your situation to support your opinion. What does it say about respect in the city? Give examples. Use linking words.

____

____

____

____

Step 4: end: What can be learned from your situation(s) or example(s)?

____

____

Step 5: Read your text again. Does it make sense? **Check** for mistakes.

More help 2 WORDS Words that form groups

____/8
▸ p. 31

Look at the words in the box. Find four words for each topic.
There are more words than you need.

admire • ~~application~~ • assistant • ~~earn~~ • cover letter • confident • necessary • reporter • application form • working hours • ~~qualities~~ • CV • stylist • ~~run out of money~~ • hotel manager • ~~jobs~~ • ~~getting on with money~~ • ~~information about work~~ • ~~budget~~ • energetic • pay • boardwalk • shift • enthusiastic • reference • reliable • breaks • ~~overspend~~

words	topic
› *earn, budget, overspend, run out of money*	› *getting on with money*
	qualities
	jobs
	information about work
	application

More help 4 WRITING An application letter

____/12
▸ p. 33

Look at the job advert and write an application letter. Write 120–180 words.

Down Under wants you

Looking for a six-month job in Australia? This is your chance!

Why not get some international experience before you start a job in your home country?
Australia City Jobs is looking for students from all over the world to work here in Australia. We have lots of different jobs waiting for you. You'll be working in one of our hotels or restaurants in one of Australia's great cities.
For example, you could be helping in the kitchen or the outdoor area, cleaning the guest rooms, working as receptionist or waiter/waitress.

What we offer you:

- 30 hours of work per week
- one or two days off every week
- good pocket money
- free accommodation and food

Write a letter of application to ACJ with details about:

- the job you're applying for
- your qualifications
- your past work experience
- the best time for you to start working
- your favourite place in Australia

Don't miss your chance! Get to know Down Under and work here at the same time!

The Manager | ACJ | Manchester Street | Sydney

You can start like this:

Dear

These phrases can help you:

Dear Mr ... / Mrs ... / Ms ...
Dear Sir/Madam
I am writing to you about ...
I saw your advert ...
I would like to apply ...
I'm good at ...
I enclose ...
Please find ... enclosed.
I'm looking forward ...
Yours faithfully/sincerely

More help **4** **LANGUAGE A job interview**

____/8

▸ p. 39/40

Megan has just had her first job interview. She wants to learn from the interview, so she writes down everything she remembers. Look at Megan's answers and fill in the questions that you think the interviewer asked her.

☞ Sieh dir immer die Antworten genau an und achte dabei besonders auf das Verb und die Zeit, in der es steht. Du musst deine Frage in dieser Zeit stellen.

interview questions	answers
What ______ ______?	My favourite subjects are science and maths.
When ______ ______?	I'm going to leave school next August.
What/Which ______ ______?	I speak French and some German.
Do ______ ______?	No, I don't. I used to play the guitar a few years ago.
What ______ ______?	My greatest strength is communication.
Do ______ ______?	Yes, I do. I work in a shoe shop every second Saturday.
Have ______ ______?	Yes, I've worked with children as a babysitter and as a volunteer at summer camps.
When ______ ______?	I can start next September.

More help 4 LANGUAGE What would have happened if …?

▸ p. 47

Conditional sentences type 3

Überlege zuerst, in welchem Teil des Satzes die Lücke ist, die du vervollständigen musst.

Ist sie im **Nebensatz** ***(if-clause)***? Dann musst du das *p___ p______* verwenden.

Ist sie im **Hauptsatz** ***(main clause)***? Dann musst du *would/could(n't)* + ____ + *past participle* verwenden.

Sowohl der Hauptsatz als auch der *if*-Satz können am Anfang oder am Ende des Satzgefüges stehen.

a) Choose the correct forms to complete the sentences (main clause). Circle them. ____/3

1 If the principal had given the students money for the new kitchen, everything had been / would have been / would be easier. (be)

2 If Mae hadn't posted pictures of the school lunch on their crowdfunding website, they wouldn't have collected / wouldn't collect / haven't collected enough money. (not collect)

3 Nothing has changed / wouldn't change / would have changed if Mae and Matteo had given up after their talk with the principal. (change)

b) Choose the correct forms to complete the sentences (if-clause). Circle them. ____/3

1 If Matteo's father wouldn't help / hadn't helped / hasn't helped them, preparing the sponsors' dinner would have taken even longer. (not help)

2 If the school lunch had been / has been / have been better, Mae wouldn't have discovered her love for cooking. (be)

3 They could have found even more sponsors if the local newspaper would report / reported / had reported on their project. (report)

More help **4 LANGUAGE In trouble**

What could they have done to get things right? Complete the sentences (conditional sentences type 3).

___/5

▸ p. 54

1 Julie forgot to call her grandma on her birthday.

If – write – the date into her calendar – remember it.

If she had written the date into her calendar, ______________________________

____

2 Jacob didn't have time to buy bread for the family.

If – not talk – with his friend Henry – have time to buy it.

____, he would have had time to buy it.

3 The Connors missed their train.

If – take a taxi – catch the train.

____, they would have caught the train.

4 I was late for my job interview.

If – get up earlier – not be late for my job interview.

If I had got up earlier, ______________________________________

____

5 Kate got a terrible cold.

If – put on a raincoat – not get a cold.

____, she wouldn't have got a cold.

Mein Lernplan

In einem Lernplan legst du fest, welche Aufgaben du an welchem Tag bearbeiten willst. Plane genügend Zeit ein und lege überschaubare „Lernportionen“ fest. Bei Unklarheiten hole Hilfe. Am Tag vor der Arbeit wiederholst du nur noch kurz. So ähnlich könnte dein Lernplan aussehen:

Datum der Klassenarbeit:	12. November
Was kommt dran?	Unit 2 (Listening, Mediation, Writing, Vokabeln, *indirect speech*)

Datum	Was ich lernen will	Erledigt?	Was ich noch einmal wiederholen muss / wichtige Hinweise
30.10.	Lernplan erstellen	✓	
31.10.	Vokabeln Unit 2 wiederholen (S. 213 – 215)	✓	Blaue Box zu *agree*!
1.11.	Vokabeln Unit 2 wiederholen (S. 216–218)	✓	
2.11.	1. *indirect speech (statements)* wiederholen (Buch, Workbook & Language file S. 192–193) 2. STOP! CHECK! GO! (Buch S. 48, Aufgabe 3 → Listening)	✓	*indirect speech (statements)* morgen noch einmal!!
3.11.	1. *indirect speech (questions, commands etc.)* wiederholen (Buch, Workbook & Language file S. 193) 2. STOP! CHECK! GO! (Buch S. 46 Aufgabe 1 b–c)	✓	
4.11.	KAT*: Klassenarbeit A (erster Teil)	✓	ganze Klassenarbeit A fertig ☺ → am 6.11. *indirect speech* wiederholen!
5.11.	PAUSE: Kino mit Florian und Lisa	✓	
6.11.	~~KAT: Klassenarbeit A (zweiter Teil)~~ *indirect speech!*	✓	*indirect speech* und Vokabeln wiederholt, mit Klassenarbeit B begonnen
7.11.	KAT: Klassenarbeit B (erster Teil)	✓	
8.11.	KAT: Klassenarbeit B (zweiter Teil)	✓	
9.11.	Alle Vokabeln wiederholen	✓	
10.11.	nur noch wiederholen (15 Minuten)	✓	noch einmal ansehen: *Mediation*
11.11.	nur noch wiederholen (15 Minuten)	✓	
12.11.	Klassenarbeit! ☺ ☺ ☺		

* KAT = *Klassenarbeitstrainer*

Datum der Klassenarbeit:	
Was kommt dran?	

Datum	Was ich lernen will	Erledigt?	Was ich noch einmal wiederholen muss / wichtige Hinweise

Datum der Klassenarbeit:	
Was kommt dran?	

Datum	Was ich lernen will	Erledigt?	Was ich noch einmal wiederholen muss / wichtige Hinweise

Bildquellen

Deutscher Verkehrssicherheitsrat (S. 26 (u. 62)); **Mark Dozier** (S. 5 unten re.); **Fotolia** (S. 9 (u. 57): Mingis; S. 32 cup: mizar_21984, wheel: Christos Georghiou, head: Co-Design, children: Trueffelpix; S. 55 re.: Balint Radu); **Ulrich Peise** (S. 27); **Shutterstock** (S. 5 oben: Monkey Business Images, unten li.: subra govinda; S. 8 li.: noBorders – Brayden Howie, re.: Filipe Frazao; S. 11: MyImages – Micha; S. 16: Jochen Schoenfeld; S. 18 li. (u. 60): DiversityStudio, re. (u. 60): iko; S. 19 oben li. (u. 60): Dora Zett, oben re. (u. 60): kostudio, unten: Lisa F. Young; S. 20 oben: racorn, unten: Burlingham; S. 23: wavebreakmedia; S. 25 Harry (u. 61): Max Topchii, Mr. Dixon (u. 61): Zurijeta, Amy (u. 61): Josep Curto, Mrs Smith (u. 61): michaeljung, Akim (u. 61): Rido, Ewa (u. 61): Piotr Marcinski; S. 29 oben li.: Rawpixel.com, oben re.: kurhan; S. 33 oben (u. 64): Tooykrub, unten (u. 64): xtock; S. 34: Zdenka Darula; S. 36: DW labs Incorporated; S. 37: Robert Kneschke; S. 39 (u. 66): Production Perig; S. 41 li.: bikeriderlondon, Mitte: Corepics VOF, re.: Robert Kneschke; S. 42 oben: oliveromg, unten: Corepics VOF; S. 44: www.BillionPhotos.com; S. 48: Rawpixel.com; S. 50: Dmitri Ma; S. 55 li.: Pitamaha)

Textquellen

S. 16 u. S. 20: Adapted from "Bullying ... What can I do?" www.respectme.org.uk/cyberbullying.html (14.06.2015). S. 24: From "Cornelsen Schulwörterbuch English G 21". Cornelsen Verlag, Berlin 2011; S. 48: Adapted from „Dein Sorgen-Tagebuch" https://www.sorgen-tagebuch.de (18.04.2016).

English G | LIGHTHOUSE 5 Klassenarbeitstrainer
Hörverstehens- und Sprechaufgaben **Gesamtlaufzeit der CD: 49'16''**

Track	Unit	Seite	Titel	Einzellaufzeit
1	Unit 1	10	Your 'Bundesland' – a place to visit?	2:01
2	Unit 1	11	Winter in Australia (Parts 1–2)	5:25
3	Unit 1	11	Winter in Australia (Part 1)	2:40
4	Unit 1	12	Winter in Australia (Part 2)	2:51
5	Unit 2	22	Improving the school climate (Part 1)	2:49
6	Unit 2	22	Improving the school climate (Part 2)	3:49
7	Unit 2	23	Improving the school climate (Part 3)	2:11
8	Unit 2	26	Making small talk	1:44
9	Unit 3	34	Training for job interviews (Part 1)	1:44
10	Unit 3	35	Training for job interviews (Part 2)	1:19
11	Unit 3	36	Work experience (Part 1)	3:23
12	Unit 3	37	Work experience (Part 2)	2:44
13	Unit 4	50	Online shopping	2:48
14	Unit 4	51	A project about advertisements (Parts 1–4)	5:53
15	Unit 4	52	A project about advertisements (Part 1)	1:45
16	Unit 4	52	A project about advertisements (Part 2)	1:23
17	Unit 4	52	A project about advertisements (Part 3)	1:47
18	Unit 4	53	A project about advertisements (Part 4)	1:24
19	Urheberrechtserklärung			0:49

Studio: Clarity Studio Berlin
Regie und Aufnahmeleitung: Christian Schmitz
Tontechnik: Christian Marx, Pascal Thinius
Sprecherinnen und Sprecher: Mala Ghedia, Marianne Graffam, Melissa Holroyd, Angus McGruther, Justin Reddig, Dharmander Singh, Darren Smith, Tomas Sinclair Spencer, Clare Wigfall, Laura Wilkinson, Ian Wood.